Contents

P9-AFR-392

Art Galleries   5
Arts Centres   21
Bookshops   30
Cinemas   36
Famous Houses and Palaces   40
Libraries   63
Museums   70
Music and Dance   112
Photographic Galleries   125
Poetry   126
Theatre   127
Annual Events and Festivals   140
Index   144
Theatres & Cinemas Map   147
Street maps   148
Underground Map   160

Introduction

Nicholson's new London Arts Guide is an introduction to the many places that house the rich variety of the capital's visual and performing arts scene. The book is practical and easy to use, with essential details such as addresses, telephone numbers and opening times set out at the head and foot of each entry. There's also useful information on whether or not you have to pay an admission charge and what refreshments are available. The chapters are divided as follows.

Art Galleries: a room-by-room guide to the great national collections; a survey of the paintings held in the smaller private galleries; notes on temporary exhibitions and some of the principal commercial galleries; plus a rundown of the major fine art auctioneers.

Arts Centres: details on the spectrum of entertainment these lively places offer under one roof.

Museums: an in-depth room-by-room guide to the giants and descriptions of the less well-known, special-interest collections.

Theatres: not only the National Theatre and West End but experimental, fringe and children's theatre; booking information – including where to get last-minute, half-price seats.

Cinemas: current release cinemas in the West End; specialists in foreign, rare and classic films.

Music and Dance: all you need to know about the Royal Opera House and the major classical music concert halls, as well as the whereabouts of rock and jazz, church music and military bands.

Famous Houses and Palaces: a preview of the unique flavour of each, from the splendours of Hampton Court to the more personal scale of Dickens' House.

Annual Events and Festivals: an original listing of reliably regular, arts-oriented happenings.

And for those in pursuit of London's literary traditions, there are sections on Bookshops, Libraries (general and specialist) and Poetry.

For the tourist, Londoner and day-visitor, here is a guide that will help you maximise your leisure time – all you have to do is go out and enjoy it.

ART GALLERIES ═══════

The three national galleries contain some of the world's finest art treasures and are an invaluable source of scholarly reference and advice. Also, they're free. In addition London has several major private collections which are open to public gaze, sometimes in exchange for an entrance fee; a few important venues for itinerant exhibitions; and, of course, the commercial galleries which are free until you decide to purchase a picture. A selection of the latter is detailed below – the area around Bond Street is a rich hunting ground for more. *Time Out*, *City Limits* and the national press carry details, and don't forget to look up the galleries at arts centres as well.

Expect to be searched on the way in and courteously deprived of items with a potential for causing malicious damage – umbrellas, especially.

NATIONAL GALLERIES

National Gallery   5 J 21

Trafalgar Sq WC2. 01-839 3321. The imposing mid-19thC building by William Wilkins houses a rich collection of important paintings, including many masterpieces. If its size daunts, pick up the excellent information sheet *A Quick Visit to the National Gallery* which directs you to 16 masterpieces, or join a guided tour which leaves the main vestibule at *11.30 from Mon–Fri*.

From the main entrance turn left to leave your coat. Turn right for stairs down to lavatories and the bright, subterranean Restaurant, *open 10.00–17.00 Mon–Sat; 14.00–17.00 Sun*, which has hot and cold drinks, wholefood snacks and luscious cakes. The Trafalgar Theatre, which opens off it, has special lectures or AV shows and details are posted outside.

Back at the main entrance go straight ahead up the stairs for the shop, *open 10.00–17.40 Mon–Sat; 14.00–17.40 Sun*, with its books, prints and postcards. A continuous AV show runs in the room marked A on the plan, and special exhibitions are mounted in rooms B and the Boardroom. There are extensive new lavatories at the Orange Street entrance.

What follows is a brief breakdown of the galleries, to be used in conjunction with the adjoining plan.

1: Early Italian and also the so-called *Wilton Diptych* in which Richard II is presented to the Virgin and Child, surrounded by angels who assure him of their support by wearing his White Hart badge.

2: Italian 15thC. Ucello, with his carousel horses.

3: Early Italian. Religious and other subjects.

4: Italian 15thC. The *Martyrdom of St Sebastian* ascribed to the Pollaiuolo brothers, the archers paired in identical poses as seen from different sides.

5: Italian 15thC. Including two Botticellis.

6: Italian 15thC. Enjoy the wonderful strip-cartoon quality of Piero de Cosimo's *Fight between the Lapiths and Centaurs*.

7: A dim and reverent sanctuary for the Leonardo cartoon.

8: Italian 16thC, Rome and Florence. Among the brilliant Raphaels don't miss the meditative tones of Leonardo's *Virgin of the Rocks*.

9: Italian 16thC, Venetian. Titian, Veronese, and Tintoretto's explosive *Origin of the Milky Way*.

10: North Italian 15thC. After the large Venetians, the smaller scale of Bellini, Montegna, Battista.

11: Italian 15thC. Altarpieces and the spiral stairway to the lower galleries.

12: North Italian 15thC. Crivelli's *Annunciation* and strikingly vivid Demidoff altarpiece.

13: North Italian 15thC. Opens directly onto the shop.

14: North Italian 16thC. Including Parmigianino's altarpiece.

15: Dutch 17thC. Rembrandt and Frans Hals.

16: Dutch 17thC. Cuyp, Jan van der Heyden, De Witte.

17: Dutch 17thC. Don't miss the fascinating detail of A. Van Ostade's *An Alchemist*.

18: Dutch 17thC. Apply the eye to Van Hoogstraten's peepshow box of a Dutch interior – from which an indignant dog stares back.

19: Dutch 17thC. The writing is on the wall at *Belshazzar's Feast* by Rembrandt – and it's not the dish of the day.

20: Flemish 17thC. Much fleshy Rubens.

21: Flemish 17thC. Dominated by a massive idealised equestrian *Charles I* by Van Dyck.

22: Flemish 17thC. More Van Dyck and Rubens, including the intensely dramatic *A Lion Hunt*.

23: German 15thC and early 16thC. Principally altarpieces.

24: Netherlandish. Van Eyck's *Arnolfini Marriage*.

25: Netherlandish 16thC and Holbein.

26: Dutch 17thC. Frans Hals and a Rembrandt or two.

27: Dutch 17thC. Van Ruisdael, Rembrandt's *Equestrian Portrait* and some reposeful Rembrandt and Frans Hals portraits.

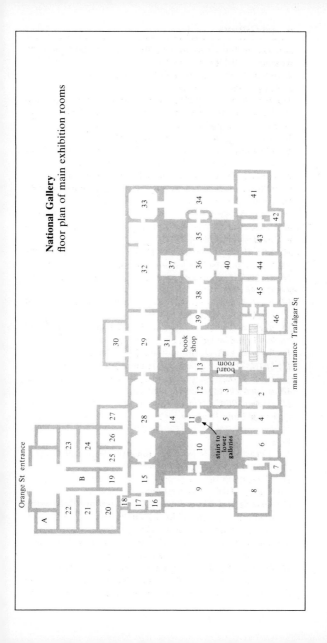

National Gallery
floor plan of main exhibition rooms

28: *Dutch 17thC.* Clear Dutch light and the tiled floors of Vermeer.

29: *Italian 17thC.* Caravaggio and Domenichino.

30: *North Italian 18thC.*

31: *Domenichino frescoes.*

32: *French 17thC.* Long bust-scattered room with Claude, Poussin, Philippe de Champaigne's sumptuous *Cardinal Richelieu* and a corner of Turners.

33: *French 18thC.* Chardin, Boucher, Watteau, Fragonard and the lustrous *Madame de Pompadour* by Drouais.

34: *Italian 18thC.* Canaletto, Guardi, Tiepolo and the wondrously laconic *Exhibition of a Rhinoceros at Venice* by Pietro Longhi.

35: *English 19thC.* Turner and Constable – the comfortable familiarity of the *Hay Wain* and the *Fighting Temeraire*, so controversial in their day.

36: *English 18thC.* Large portraits – a Reynolds, a Gainsborough and Lawrence's arresting *Queen Charlotte*.

37: *Italian 17thC.* Dominated by the collection's largest picture – Guido Reni's *Adoration of the Shepherds.*

38: *English 18thC.* Reynolds, Gainsborough, Stubbs and four episodes from Hogarth's *Marriage à la Mode.*

39: *English 18thC.* Stubbs, Gainsborough and Hogarth's *Marriage Contract.*

40: *French 19thC.* Delicate little Corots and Courbets.

41: *Spanish.* Goya's *Duke of Wellington*, El Greco, Velasquez, Murillo.

42: A tiny corner of Goya paintings.

43: *French 19thC.* Delacroix, Ingres and Moreau's jewel-like *George and the Dragon.*

44: *French 19thC.* Pissarro, Manet, Monet, Sisley, Degas, Renoir.

45: *French 19thC.* Seurat's *Bathers*, Rousseau's *Tiger*, Cézanne's *Bathers* and Picasso's *Child with a Dove*. Plus Van Gogh's *Sunflowers.*

46: *French 19thC.* Mainly Monet's *Waterlilies.*

Lower Galleries: Here the centrepiece is a neat little series of showcases on the development of the gallery. For the rest, paintings in heavy gilt frames hang two or three deep on walls and screens. This is the overflow, not only the dubious in quality and provenance but also lesser known works of top artists. You feel you are exploring the well-lit storerooms of a major art collector – and so you are.

Open 10.00–18.00 Mon–Sat; 14.00–18.00 Sun. Closed some Nat Hols. Free.

National Portrait Gallery 5 J 22

2 St Martin's Pl WC2. 01-930 1552. Fascinating collection of contemporary portraits of major figures in British history. The gallery is unique in that the subjects are more important than the quality of the painting – you will frequently encounter the works of important artists in appealing juxta-position with unskilled but possibly lifelike watercolours.

On entering, turn left and down a short flight of stairs to the bookstall with its reproductions, prints, cards, books and guide books. Return to the vestibule and leave coats and umbrellas towards the back left of the lobby. Stairs to the right of the lobby lead down to the basement, where there are usually one or two small exhibitions, including one on recent acquisitions, and the lavatories. There are no refreshments – try the National Gallery next door.

You are free to wander at will, but the curators recommend you to take the lift to the top floor and work your way down through history until the main doors evict you into the present (usually at the feet of some itinerant artists who will capture your own likeness for a small fee).

Start with the only numerical mistake, on the upper mezzanine.

26: The Middle Ages. Portrait of Richard II, electrotypes of royal tomb effigies and reproductions from illustrated manuscripts.

1: The Tudors. Sumptuous and dramatic – Henry VIII, Elizabeth I, William Shakespeare and contemporaries.

2: The Stuarts. Paintings of James I and the Civil War in a room lightly garnished with armour. Don't miss the *Self-Portrait* by Van Dyck.

3: The enquiring mind – an electrotype of an effigy of Sir Francis Bacon sleeps under the heading. Here also are John Evelyn, Newton, Milton and miniatures of thinkers.

4: The self-congratulatory curled wigs of the **Restoration**.

5: Queen Anne in the company of the Duchess of Marlborough and contemporary earls.

6: Early 18thC arts and sciences. Pope, Vanbrugh, Congreve.

7: The titled members of the Kit-Cat Club, a group of leading Whigs of the 18thC, painted by Sir Godfrey Kneller.

8: Georges I and II and their contemporaries. Wesley, Handel, Hogarth's *Self-Portrait*.

9: The arts in the 18thC. Laurence Sterne, a bust of Colley Cibber, Reynolds' *Self-Portrait*.

10: Britain overseas. The impact of Clive of India and the voyages of Captain Cook.

11: The struggle for America, and John Singleton Copley's massive *Death of the Earl of Chatham*, equipped with a key to aid in the identification of its famous subjects.

12: Britain at war. Another vast set-piece, *France Declares War on England: Pitt Addresses the Commons* by Karl Anton Hichel.

13: The Romantics, with a dreamily romantic centrepiece of Edward William Lane in Arabic dress. Here, too, are Wordsworth, Southey, Coleridge, Shelley, Byron, Burns *et alia.*

14: Science and the Industrial Revolution. Edward Jenner is here and James Watt, Brunel, Telford and Macadam – he of the well-known road surface.

15: The Regency. Don't let Beechey's *Admiral Lord Nelson,* Romney's *Lady Hamilton* and Lawrence's *George IV* blind you to the small watercolour of Jane Austen by her sister, the only authentic likeness of her.

16A: Kept for special, important exhibitions on changing themes, usually on loan from elsewhere, usually with an entrance charge.

16: The young Victoria.

17: The early Victorians. Pay homage to Edmund Kean, the Brontës, Dickens, Tennyson and the aesthetic figures of the Oxford Movement.

18: Poverty and the people. Peel, Bentinck and an engraving of the *Meeting of the Council of the Anti-Corn Law League.*

19 & 23: Two halves of a single long gallery entitled *The Empire and the later Victorians.* The daunting stare of Kitchener, the horrors of the Indian Mutiny and *Captain Frederick Burnaby* by James Tissot.

20: Victorian technology. Stephenson and the railways, Prince Albert and the Great Exhibition.

21: Victorian writers and artists. The Brownings and Swinburne are there but don't miss, high above a door, Landseer working on a lion destined for Trafalgar Square.

22: Lecture room. Free seasons of lectures are conducted at *11.00 on Tue* and *15.30 on Sat* during term times.

24 & 25: Edwardian arts and politics. Beardsley, Thomas Hardy and Ellen Terry, Emmeline Pankhurst, Rupert Brooke, the Bloomsbury Group and, of course, Edward VII.

27: Mezzanine floor. *The First World War,* dominated by upright figures in khaki with a small corner given over to the war poets.

Upper ground: *Modern Royal portraits* – Annigoni's portrait of Elizabeth II and Organ's controversial *Diana, Princess of Wales and Prince Charles.*

Ground Floor: *The 20thC.* The display was still under construction at the time of going to press, but it will be large and will contain space for small temporary exhibitions of prints and photographs to keep the exhibition fully up to date. *Open 10.00–17.00 Mon–Fri; 10.00–18.00 Sat; 14.00–18.00 Sun. Closed Nat Hols. Free – occasional charge for special exhibitions.*

Tate Gallery   **5 P 18**
Millbank SW1. 01-821 1313. This is the home of the bulk of the national collection of British art and the national collection of modern art. It complements the National Gallery – repository of the national collection of European Old Masters – exhibiting important British paintings in order to give an overall view of European art.

The Gallery was born in 1889 when Sir Henry Tate, of Tate and Lyle sugar, bequeathed his collection of British paintings to the nation. The imposing classical building, designed by Sidney R.J. Smith, has been extended twice since its opening in 1897 and is still short of space for its unrivalled and ever-growing collection. The curators perform a kind of intelligent juggling act with the priceless works in their care in order to keep them passing before the eyes of the public and to ensure that nothing stays hidden in store for too long. For this reason it would be misleading to attempt a detailed gallery by gallery guide.

Go up the steps to the central hall. Turn right for the cloakroom where coats may (and umbrellas must) be left. Then turn left to the shop where, as well as the chance to buy art books and reproductions of pictures, you can pick up a free single-sheet plan to guide you to the current arrangement of works. Just past the shop, signs direct you down to the lavatories, telephones, the smart self-service coffee shop (*open 10.30–17.30 Mon–Sat; 14.00–17.30 Sun*) and the classier, pricier but quite excellent restaurant (*open 12.00–15.00 Mon–Sat*). This serves traditional English food, sometimes from 17thC recipes, and it is wise to book on 01-834 6754.

There follows an indication of some of the artists and works of art you may expect to encounter on any visit:

British Collection
16th and 17thC painting. Elizabethan portraits, *Man in a Black Cap* by John Bettes, dated 1545 and the earliest work here. Very English views of Henley and Hampton Court.

18thC painting. Gainsborough (notice the ghostly original horse's head beginning to show through in his *A Market Cart*). Hogarth, including the *Graham Children* and his *Self-Portrait*. Romantic landscapes by P.J. de Loutherbourg. Reynolds, including self-portraits. Romney. Stubbs' horses in painful encounters with lions. Joseph Wright of Derby's *An Experiment with the Air Pump*.

Early 19thC painting. William Blake's muscular, mystical illustrations and the works of followers, Samuel Palmer, George Richmond, Edward Calvert. Constable's lush landscapes and fine portraits. Swirls of angels and scenes from Shakespeare by Fuseli. Landseer, including the *Hunted Stag*, Thomas Lawrence, and an unmatchable collection of the works of Turner.

The Pre-Raphaelites. Here are Millais and Rossetti, Ford Maddox Brown, Holman Hunt, Arthur Hughes, Burne-Jones' *King Cophetua and the Beggar-Maid*, Millais' *Boyhood of Raleigh*.

Late Victorian and Edwardian painting. Aubrey Beardsley, the nightmarish *Fairy Feller's Master-Stroke* by Richard Dadd, Lord Leighton, John S. Sargent's portraits, including *Monet Painting*, Sickert, Tissot, G.F. Watts and Whistler, including most of his *Nocturnes*.

Modern Collection

20thC painting and sculpture. Works by Winston Churchill, the Camden Town Group, Francis Bacon, the Euston Road School, Duncan Grant, Augustus and Gwen John, Wyndham Lewis, including his portraits of Pound and Edith Sitwell, David Hockney, Matisse, Picasso and Braque, L.S. Lowry, Ben Nicolson, John Piper, Stanley Spencer, Graham Sutherland. Sculptures by Giacometti, Gabo, Hepworth, Moore, Rodin.

Impressionist and Post-Impressionist. Sisley, Pissarro, Van Gogh, Gauguin, Cezanne, Monet, Manet, Bonnard, Seurat, the *Little Dancer* by Degas and all.

You will also find examples of Surrealism, European Abstraction and Expressionism, a Mark Rothko room, American Expressionism, Op Art, Pop Art, Abstract Art, Minimal and Conceptual Art (the last two new enough still to be highly controversial).

There are regular lectures, either in the lecture theatre in the lower galleries or in the public galleries themselves, free guided tours and a regular monthly programme of films on art and art history. Although the gallery is free, a regular visitor might consider buying a subscription to become a

Friend of the Tate for special admission at times when it is normally closed to the public, invitations to private views and free admission to the occasional special exhibition for which there is a charge.
Open 10.00–18.00 Mon–Sat; 14.00–18.00 Sun. Closed Nat Hols. Free.

PERMANENT COLLECTIONS

Courtauld Institute Galleries   3 F 24
Woburn Sq WC1. 01-580 1015. Pay on the ground floor and then rise in a large and rackety lift to the top floor where a series of rooms opening out of one another contain Samuel Courtauld's own bequest, the collection of Lord Lee of Fareham, the Roger Fry bequest of 19thC and 20thC British and French paintings, the Witt collection of Old Master drawings and the Gambier-Parry bequest of early Italian paintings, each with a separate catalogue. The exhibition changes from time to time partly because they have more pictures than wall space and partly because material is offered on loan for specialist exhibitions elsewhere. However you are certain to be confronted by Botticelli, Rubens, Rembrandt, Tiepolo, Goya and an important collection of French Impressionist and Post-Impressionist works. *Open 10.00–17.00 Mon–Sat; 14.30–18.00 Sun. Closed Nat Hols. Charge.*

Dulwich Picture Gallery
College Rd SE21. 01-693 5254. England's first purpose-built art gallery, and surely one of the most tranquil and pleasant, in an almost rural setting. Much admired by Robert Browning and John Ruskin among others. Designed by Sir John Soane with natural light washing down from above and incorporating a mausoleum for the benefactors which is bathed in amber light and has a slightly eerie sense of expectancy. The collection includes important works by Rembrandt, Rubens, Gainsborough, Cuyp, Watteau, Murillo, Poussin, Hogarth and Van Dyck and the only known portrait of Richard Burbage.
Buy ticket, books and cards in the entrance hall with its exhibition on the gallery's history. Then turn left and walk to the far end to begin at room 1.
1: Gainsborough portraits of the musical Linley family.
2: Dutch and Flemish pictures, dominated by Reynolds' *Mrs Siddons*.
3: Outstanding portraits – Rubens, Lely, Hogarth.

4: 17thC paintings from Spain, Italy and France.

5: 18thC paintings from the South.

6: Dutch – especially Cuyp whose cows always seem larger than anyone else's.

7: Small and charming cabinet pictures from Holland.

8: Italian and French paintings and some Rubens sketches, a few of doubtful provenance.

9: 18thC and 19thC English portraits, including Reynolds' *Self.*

10: 17thC English and Dutch.

11: The cream of the *Dutch collection,* including three Rembrandts.

12: 17thC views of Rome. Rich in Poussins.

It is worth lingering in the gardens to pay respects to the distinguished and venerable trees – a Judas tree, a gingko, two mulberries and a tulip tree.

Open 10.00–13.00; 14.00–17.00 Tue–Sat; 14.00–17.00 Sun. Closed Mon & Nat Hols. Charge.

Heinz Gallery   **2 D 17**

RIBA Drawings Collection, 21 Portman Sq W1. 01-580 5533. The Royal Institute of British Architects' extensive collection of drawings may be viewed by appointment from *10.00–13.00 Mon–Thu*, and from time to time appear in their public exhibitions, arranged around specific themes. *Open 10.00–20.00 Mon–Thu; 10.00–18.00 Fri & Sat; 12.00–18.00 Sun. Closed between exhibitions. Charge.*

Ranger's House

Chesterfield Wlk, Blackheath SE10. 01-853 0035. The attractive late 17thC villa, once home of the 4th Earl of Chesterfield and later of General Lord Wolsey, is famous for the Suffolk collection of paintings. Hire a catalogue in the entrance hall and then wander through the spacious, airy rooms with their long windows looking on to the lush greenery of Greenwich Park. Ladies and gentlemen of Stuart and Jacobean England gaze down from the walls, dressed in much lace and painted in such intricate detail that they serve as invaluable reference material on contemporary court dress. Suitable furniture is gradually being acquired to stand beneath them – a massive pair of 18thC giltwood tables is already in place. Eventually the upper rooms will house the Dolmetsch collection of antique musical instruments, presently at the Horniman Museum. Study facilities for schools are in the basement. *Open 10.00–17.00 Mon–Sun. Free.*

Royal College of Music Department of Portraits   **1 G 10**
Prince Consort Rd SW7. 01-589 3643, Ext 23. Tucked away
in one of the towers of the College is a small exhibition of
various kinds of pictorial representations of musicians – oils,
watercolours, prints, photographs, busts, from the 16thC to
the present day. The most famous pictures – Haydn by
Hardy, 1791, and one of only two known portraits of Elgar
(this one by Talbot) are always on show. For the rest it's a
rotating display because they don't have space to show
everything at once. There is also a collection of ephemera
which includes not only conductors batons, musicians personal effects and illustrated title pages of printed music but
also the largest collection of concert programmes in the
country, more than 83,000 of them. An appointment is
essential. Special items in store can usually be produced,
research facilities are readily available and reproductions are
on sale. *Open 10.00–17.00 Mon–Fri, by appointment only.*
Free.

TEMPORARY EXHIBITIONS

B2
Metropolitan Wharf, Wapping Wall El. 01-488 9815. 6,000
square feet of moveable space in an ex-warehouse devoted
to new work in the spheres of painting, photography, film,
video and even performance art – although with a strong
emphasis on the visual arts. No refreshments, but the area is
strong on cafés and pubs. *Open 13.00–18.00 Tue–Sun.*
Closed Mon. Charge.

Bankside Gallery   **6 N 26**
48 Hopton St SE1. 01-928 7521. Attractive gallery on the
refurbished waterfront that is the home of the Royal Society
of Painters in Watercolours and the Royal Society of
Painter-Etchers and Engravers, who exhibit twice a year.
Also mounts prestige exhibitions and retrospectives. There
is sometimes a charge, and the pictures are sometimes for
sale. *Open 10.00–17.00 Tue–Sat; 14.00–18.00 Sun. Closed*
Mon, Nat Hols and between exhibitions.

Camden Arts Centre
Arkwright Rd NW3. 01-435 2643. Above the school with its
day and evening classes in the fine arts, there are three
galleries, almost always offering three separate exhibitions,
and closing only briefly during changeovers. All the visual
arts are represented at one time or another – and in summer
don't miss the sculpture displays in the garden. The students'

restaurant, *10.00–16.00 Mon–Fri*, is open to the public, and the bookshop has posters, magazines and a wide range of art books. *Open 11.00–18.00 Mon–Sat, to 20.00 Fri; 14.00–18.00 Sun. Free.*

Guildhall Art Gallery 6 M 30

Aldermanbury EC2. 01-606 3030. Approach by way of Guildhall Square and you will encounter the separate entrance to the gallery on your right. Here two floors of exhibition space display the works of professional artists in a programme of 10 or 12 different shows throughout the year. The pictures are usually for sale. *Opening times vary. Closed between exhibitions. Free.*

Hayward Gallery 6 M 23

South Bank SE1. 01-928 3144. The gallery can be picked out from the rest of the South Bank complex by the kinetic sculpture it wears on its head. Its two floors of exhibition space are administered by the Arts Council who mount major changing exhibitions of British, American and European art. No permanent exhibition. The small bookshop in the entrance hall also sells postcards and prints relevant to the current exhibition. *Open 10.00–20.00 Mon–Thu; 10.00–18.00 Fri & Sat; 12.00–18.00 Sun. Charge.*

Mall Galleries 5 K 21

Carlton House Ter, The Mall SW1. 01-930 6844. The galleries of the Federation of British Artists whose 15 member art societies, including some royal societies, exhibit new work, usually for sale. Sometimes hired out to other bodies. *Open (usually) 10.00–17.00 Mon–Sat. Closed Sun & between exhibitions. Charge.*

Orleans House Gallery

Riverside, Twickenham, Middx. 01-892 0221. The gallery has been converted from a partially demolished 18thC house designed by James Gibbs, with its dramatic central octagon room preserved intact. The original house acquired its name in 1815 when the exiled Louis Phillipe, Duke of Orleans, stayed in it for two years. It was given to the borough of Twickenham by its last private owner, Mrs Nellie Ionides, whose collection of local paintings are exhibited a few at a time due to lack of space (though you may certainly see the rest by appointment). The temporary exhibitions may feature the work of local artists but are often of more general interest – travelling Arts Council exhibitions of painting and photography, for example. Anyway, it's on a lovely part of the river. *Open 13.00–17.30 Tue–Sat; 14.00–17.30 Sun & Nat Hols. Closed mornings, Mon, Good Fri & Christmas. Free.*

Queen's Gallery   **5 K 17**
Buckingham Palace, Buckingham Palace Rd SW1. 01-930 4832 Ext 351. A discreet side entrance, with an awning to keep the rain off the queue, opens first on to a long passageway lined with framed prints, all for sale. The passage leads to the exhibition itself, displayed in one room with a gallery, formerly a private chapel. Here the priceless paintings and drawings of the Royal collection are hung in small, changing exhibitions, carefully planned so that most of the works of art in the vast and important collection are made available to the public gaze at some time or another, together with occasional pieces of superb furniture. *Open 11.00–17.00 Tue–Sat; 14.00–17.00 Sun. Closed Mon. Charge.*

Royal Academy of Fine Arts   **2 I 19**
Burlington House, Piccadilly W1. 01-734 9052. The original house was redesigned in 1715 by the 3rd Earl of Burlington, an architect and effective patron of the arts, but the imposing Piccadilly frontage is the work of R.R. Banks and S.M. Barry. Much dignified research and study is engaged upon on the upper floors and in the two wings because this is the HQ of the Society of Antiquaries, the Geological Society, the Royal Society of Chemistry, the Royal Astronomical Society and the Linnean Society. But these rooms are private, as are many of the rooms belonging to the Royal Academy of Fine Arts itself. What is important to the visitor is the series of major special loan exhibitions held throughout the year, always containing works by major artists and often putting before the public pictures that could not otherwise be seen because they are in private collections. Of lesser importance is the perhaps more famous Summer Exhibition, from May to Aug, in which the work of living artists is displayed.
The sculpture in the entrance quadrangle is of the founder, Sir Joshua Reynolds (by Alfred Drury). The front hall has the cloakroom, tickets and guides; lavatories and shop and the spacious exhibition galleries themselves lie at the top of the wide stairway. *Open 10.00–18.00 Mon–Sun. Charge.*

Serpentine Gallery   **1 F 11**
Kensington Gardens W8. 01-402 6075. The old Kensington Gardens tea house is a lovely setting for a variety of

exhibitions of contemporary art – painting, sculpture, photography *et alia* – which change monthly. Because it is in a Royal park, closing time is brought forward in winter when the park is shut at dusk. It also sometimes closes between exhibitions. There is a tiny bookshop in the lobby. No refreshments these days, but the Serpentine restaurant, buffet and bars are only a duck's waddle away. *Open 10.00– 18.00 Mon–Sun in summer; 10.00–dusk in winter. Free.*

South London Art Gallery
Peckham Rd SE5. 01-703 6120. The small but interesting collection of the work of British artists from 1700, including several pictures of local relevance, is in store, but is brought forth in the form of temporary exhibitions from time to time. Specific paintings can be viewed on application at other times. For the rest, it houses varied temporary exhibitions including, sometimes, work from the adjoining art school. *Open 10.00–18.00 Tue–Sat; 15.00–18.00 Sun. Closed Mon & between exhibitions. Free.*

Whitechapel Art Gallery
80 Whitechapel High St E1. 01-377 0107. One of the liveliest and most exciting of them all. Its two floors of flexible exhibition space are used for changing displays of contemporary art – painting, sculpture and photography. Art books, posters and magazines are on sale in the foyer and the tiny cinema usually offers a continuous audio-visual show on one or more of the current exhibitions. The vegetarian snacks and sticky cakes that seem to go with the London arts scene are available in the cafeteria. Don't get run over as you step back outside to admire the slightly off-centre Art Nouveau frontage. *Closed for renovation in 1984. Re-opening 1985. Ring for details.*

COMMERCIAL GALLERIES

Agnew   2 I 19
43 Old Bond St W1. 01-629 6176. Outstanding selection of old masters and changing exhibitions of established British contemporary painters. *Open 09.30–17.30 Mon–Fri. Closed Sat.*

Angela Flowers   2 F 22
11 Tottenham Mews W1. 01-637 3089. Exciting exhibitions of work by younger British artists – nothing earlier than 1952. Also run a popular print-of-the-month club from which members must pick four prints per year. *Open 10.30– 18.00 Tue–Fri; 10.30–12.30 Sat. Closed Mon.*

Crane Kalman   **1 I 11**
178 Brompton Rd SW3. 01-584 7566. Specialists in 20thC
British and European paintings. You may cast your eyes
over works by Nicolson, Moore, Sutherland, Degas and
Dufy. *Open 10.00–18.00 Mon–Fri; 10.00–16.00 Sat.*

Curwen Gallery   **2 F 22**
4 Windmill St, off Charlotte St W1. 01-636 1459. Originals
and prints by younger British artists – Chloe Cheese,
Christopher Corr, Paul Ryan – and prints by well-known
sculptors – Moore, Hepworth and Frink amongst them.
Open 10.00–18.00 Tue–Fri; 11.00–16.00 Sat. Closed Mon.

Editions Graphiques   **2 H 19**
3 Clifford St W1. 01-734 3944. Arts Deco and Nouveau
prints, paintings, pottery, sculpture, glass, jewellery, silver
and furniture. Also Symbolist pictures, graphics right across
the board, and relevant books. *Open 10.00–18.00 Mon–Fri;
10.00–14.00 Sat.*

Gimpel Fils   **2 G 18**
30 Davies St W1. 01-493 2488. Contemporary art in various
forms from Britain, the rest of Europe and America. *Open
09.30–17.30 Mon–Fri; 10.00–13.00 Sat.*

Malcolm Innes   **4 J 11**
172 Walton St SW3. 01-584 0575. Paintings, prints and
watercolours of a Scottish and sporting persuasion. You will
find Landseers, Ansdells and Farquharsons and 20thC bird
pictures. *Open 09.30–18.00 Mon–Fri. Closed Sat.*

Marlborough Fine Art   **2 I 19**
6 Albemarle St W1. 01-629 5161. Selected old masters, fine
Impressionist and 20thC paintings, drawings and sculptures.
And original graphic works of art and photographs by
leading 20thC artists. *Open 10.00–17.30 Mon–Fri; 10.00–
12.30 Sat.*

Waddington   **2 H 19**
2 Cork St W1. 01-439 1866. Paintings, drawings, watercolours and sculpture from 20thC English, American and
Continental artists, and a separate department for contemporary prints. *Open 10.00–17.30 Mon–Fri; 10.00–13.00
Sat.*

FINE ART AUCTIONEERS

It is fascinating and free to view what's on offer at the sale
rooms but only the initiated should risk a bid where high

prices and high speed reign. See *The Daily Telegraph* on Mon and *The Times* on Tue for details of previews.

W. & F. C. Bonham & Sons   2 I 12

Montpelier Galleries, Montpelier St SW7. 01-584 9161. Oils and watercolours, Oriental works of art, clocks, silver, porcelain, furniture and jewellery are on offer. Painting sales at *11.00 on Thu*. Especially appealing are the occasional evening 'theme' auctions (dog paintings to coincide with Crufts, for example) with wine served to set the mood beforehand. *Open 09.00–17.30 Mon–Fri.*

Christie, Manson & Woods   5 J 19

8 King St, St James's SW1. 01-839 9060. Internationally famous and fully comprehensive fine art auctioneers in

A London art auction

whose premises works of art and large sums of money have regularly changed hands since 1766. Sales generally begin at *11.00 and continue after lunch. Open 09.00–16.45 Mon–Fri.*

Christie's South Kensington   **1 I 9**
58 Old Brompton Rd SW7. 01-581 2231. A slightly down-market younger brother of the St James's branch, dealing in toys, cars, jewellery, wine and furs. *Open 09.00–19.00 Mon; 09.00–16.45 Tue–Fri.*

Phillips   **2 G 19**
7 Blenheim St, New Bond St W1. 01-629 6602. Fine art sales every morning which include furniture, silver, ceramics, paintings and prints. Special collectors' sales at *12.00 on Wed* (lead soldiers, photos and the like). Their Marylebone Auction Rooms at Hayes Pl, Lisson Grove NW1, 01-723 2647 offer pictures and modern household effects at *10.00 on Fri* and the branch at 10 Salem Rd W2, 01-221 5303 specialises in Victorian and Edwardian furniture and works of art at *10.00 on Thu. All open 08.30–17.00 Mon–Fri; 08.30–12.00 Sat.*

Sotheby's Parke Bernet   **2 G 19**
34-35 New Bond St W1. 01-493 8080. Began as rare book specialists but are now world-famous for disposing of everything that comes under the headings of antiques and works of art – and with a turnover that runs easily into millions of pounds. *Open 09.00–16.30 Mon-Fri.*

ARTS CENTRES ════════

These are among the liveliest and most exciting of London's arts venues. Each offers several different kinds of entertainment under one roof – theatre, music, exhibitions – often of a new and experimental nature. Some run classes where you can study arts related subjects very cheaply. Some set up workshops to encourage participation in various aspects of the performing arts. Most are funded by the Arts Council and the GLC or local boroughs. All offer food and drink of some kind. Even if you do no more than attend a single performance of a play you can't help but be aware of the sense of energy and creativity generated by the other activities.

Time Out and *City Limits* carry details of performances

and the Barbican is advertised in the London and national press, but it is often worth a telephone call to find out about events arranged at short notice. Note that some centres require membership (and full membership brings regularly mailed information and cheaper tickets) but one-day membership is readily and cheaply available on the spot.

Africa Centre   6 J 23
38 King St WC2. 01-836 1973. An active arts centre in the heart of Covent Garden running a series of courses, in conjunction with the School of Oriental and African Studies, for all who wish to study African languages, politics and dance. Information from the resource centre, where the library is too. The art gallery, whose exhibitions change monthly, offers free exhibition space to artists from Africa and the less developed countries and the bookshop is exclusively stocked with works by African writers and books on Africa.
The hall, with stage and lighting facilities, is available by day for conferences on relevant topics and is frequently hired by peripatetic groups bringing film shows, plays, or music and dance to liven up the evenings.
Dishes from many parts of Africa are on offer in the Calabash restaurant and there is a small separate bar for those who fancy a jar. The centre is open to all, but membership brings priority booking facilities and price concessions. Gallery, classes and bookshop *open 09.30–17.30 Mon–Sat; hall open for events; restaurant and bar open 12.00–15.00 & 18.00–23.00 Mon–Sat; closed Sat lunch.*

Barbican Centre   6 K 30
Barbican EC2. Admin: 01-638 4141. Recorded information on events: 01-628 9760. Box office: 01-628 8795. Credit card bookings: 01-638 8891. Rising out of war-devastated acres, this walled city within the City – ten years in the building and opened in 1982 – is notorious for the size and complexity of its design and for the impression it gives of walling the arts in and the rest of us out. However, don't be deterred, as it is well worth the trouble of penetrating its exterior for the treasures within. But do allow time to reach seats before performances begin and do pick up the free guide booklet 'Welcome to the Barbican Centre'. Note the massive geometric, shining steel sculpture lighting the main staircase. The Barbican Theatre, reached from levels 3–6, is the home of the Royal Shakespeare Company who present their

master's works in repertory, as well as other classics, and modern drama. A breathtaking stainless steel safety curtain, curved like folds of material, falls in intervals. Seats are comfortable, but the aisleless rows are off-putting if you want to get out in a hurry for any reason. Below, on level 1, is the small studio theatre, the Pit, where they offer more informal productions of classical and new plays.

The Barbican Hall on levels 5 and 6 is the home of the London Symphony Orchestra and also plays host to classical music and light entertainment from other sources. Hundreds of perspex globes hang from the ceiling as acoustical aids. Decorative wood block floors extend throughout and into the foyer, around bars so long that you should feel confident of being served quickly.

The Art Gallery was not designed as such and is the least successful space in use in the centre. On two floors, reached from level 8, it is sometimes given over to major exhibitions or can hold two or more smaller ones. On occasion the open-air Sculpture Court, on the same level, is involved also.

Cinema 1, on level 1, aims to be a 'local', showing current general releases, but intersperses them with important films which may not get a showing elsewhere. Cinemas 2 and 3, on level 9, are principally for conferences but sometimes used as back-up to Cinema 1.

The Library, level 7, is the HQ of the City lending library service, with the emphasis on the arts. Members of other UK public libraries may borrow books, others must peruse them in situ.

Apart from its luxury City-gent accommodation the centre has conference facilities, the City Business School, the Guildhall School of Music and Drama, a variety of exhibitions on matters of interest to the City (crime prevention, for example, or food) in the exhibition halls reached from a walkway on level 8, and frequent free entertainment in the foyers.

Sustenance is available on several levels, in all senses. The Cut Above licensed restaurant, on level 7, serves full meals between *12.00–15.00 and from 18.00 until 30 minutes after last performance* (book on 01-588 3008). The Waterside Café on level 5 is a self-service coffee, salad and wine bar, with seating inside and out, overlooking the artificial lake and is *open 10.00–20.00 Mon–Sat; 12.00–20.00 Sun & Nat Hols*. Bars, coffee and snack bars on levels 1, 3, 5 and 6 are open for performances. *Centre open every day. For performance times see daily press.*

Battersea Arts Centre
Old Town Hall, Lavender Hill SW11. Admin 01-223 6557/8/9. Box office 01-223 8413. A friendly, active community centre with as many volunteer helpers as regular staff. The small cinema (ground floor, turn left) shows a mixture of foreign, classic and 'general-release-you've-just-missed' films, usually grouped in themes. The adaptable theatre (first floor, turn right) accommodates a lively mix of visiting fringe theatre, dance companies, mime artists, rock, jazz and folk musicians. There are children's films on Sat afternoon and live shows on Sun afternoon. The gallery (first floor, right through the bar) holds changing exhibitions of paintings by local artists, almost always for sale. The bookshop (ground floor, turn right) has an excellent stock of radical and feminist books, 'quality' literature, children's books, books on the visual arts, magazines and quirky greetings cards.

Every Sun there's a craft market in the main entrance hall

and five or six times a year a festival (dance festival, fiddle festival) sweeps through the whole centre with relevant films, music and even books on sale.

There is a huge variety of day and evening classes and workshops, some specifically for adults, some for children, some for family groups. Emphasis is on dance and music. A crèche is provided for women taking classes in self-defence and exercise. The fully-equipped pottery has three resident potters and there is also a photographic workshop and darkroom.

The licensed café, serving home-made and partly vegetarian food is open all week and the bar, with its locally brewed real ale, from Wed–Sun at the usual licensing hours. *Open 10.00–23.00 Mon–Sat; 10.00–22.30 Sun* (but most activities are Wed–Sun). *Bookshop open 11.30–21.30 Wed–Sun.*

Cockpit Theatre

Gateforth St NW8. 01-262 7907. A purpose-built youth arts workshop, with compact spaces intensively used by secondary school children, students and the young unemployed, who sometimes spill over into the Holborn annexe for classes or workshops. Its principal aims are the admirable ones of promoting the arts as a teaching-aid in schools and colleges of further education, and involving the local community in video, drama, photography, poetry, theatre and visual arts workshops.

However, the centre around which the whole thing revolves, and which has the widest impact, is the adaptable studio theatre, where avant-garde drama and music is offered by both professional and amateur visiting companies. They also tend to set up musical and dramatic events in unexpected parts of town – on Clapham Common for example – which are always worth a visit.

The small foyer has a bar and light snacks, seating, and changing exhibitions of student art on the walls. The distant throb comes from the beat of the electronic music workshop, above. *Open 09.00–22.30 Mon–Sun; closed two weeks at Christmas, two weeks in Jul. Bar open licensing hours.*

Commonwealth Institute   1 D 5

230 Kensington High St W8. 01-603 4535. Behind a forest of flagpoles stands what appears to be a glass and concrete tent, erected in the early 60s for this centre of information about the Commonwealth and its member nations. The inside of the building is encircled by three levels of exhibition galleries with models, dioramas and objects, arranged by

theme, to illustrate the cultural and economic life not only of the Commonwealth countries but of the continents of Asia and Africa as well. These galleries are open-sided so wherever you are you can look across the central space and see what is below or round the opposite side.

On the first floor signs point to an art gallery, and to the library and resource centre with book exhibitions and facilities for study, and the quick information centre.

To the west is the arts centre, reached from the exhibition building or through its own entrance from the car park. Here the bar – with real ale, coffee and snacks as well as the usual drinks – leads to the box office and the stairs down to the theatre where music, drama, dance and films (on the roll-down screen) are on offer regularly and often free.

Schools and adult groups are catered for with special talks, tours and information packs, all free, and the entire place breaks into noisy life from time to time with a festival or carnival arranged by one particular country. Don't miss the book and gift shop near the main entrance or the Bhownagree gallery downstairs, with its regular art exhibitions. Flags restaurant (01-602 3063) is run on the lines of a hotel coffee shop with snacks always available and hot meals at lunchtime. *Open 10.00–17.30 Mon–Sat; 14.00–17.30 Sun. Closed Nat. Hols. Free, with charge to cover cost of special exhibitions. Bar open 11.00–15.00 Mon–Sat. Restaurant open 10.00–17.00 Mon–Sat; 14.00–16.30 Sun.*

French Institute   **1 I 9**
17 Queensberry Pl SW7. 01-589 6211. Cultural activities for French-speaking – or anyway French-understanding – people. Membership brings obvious benefits – cheaper tickets, mailed information, the freedom to take books out of the extensive library. However, anyone may buy a ticket for a film (French, sometimes with English subtitles), a lecture on some aspect of French cultural life, a theatrical event or a concert. Anyone may consult the 70,000 French language books or the current magazines and newspapers in situ, rubbing shoulders with students from the nearby Lycée Français, or walk around the spacious gallery admiring the changing exhibitions of works by French artists or of France. Don't be so eager to get inside that you neglect to admire the decorative exterior of the mid-30s building, designed in collaboration by a Frenchman and an Englishman, M. Bonnet and Mr Thomas, and opened just before the Second World War.
No refreshments. *Open 10.00–20.00 Mon; 10.00–18.00 Tue–Fri; 10.00–13.00 Sat. Library open 11.00.*

ICA (Institute of Contemporary Arts)   **5 K 20**
12 Carlton House Ter SW1. 01-930 0493. Recorded information: 01-930 6393. In the foyer you will find the booking office, magazine and postcard stands and a small but well-stocked bookshop – mostly paperbacks on visual or performing arts subjects, quality contemporary literature and Virago revivals. To go further you must buy a day membership ticket, unless you have already taken out annual membership.
At any one time there are three exhibitions of paintings, drawings, architects' plans or photography held in the main gallery to the right, the concourse gallery which leads to restaurant and theatre, and the upper gallery.
The cinema screens foreign, avant-garde and unusual films (a Dracula season, for example) in the evenings and at

weekend matinees, and there is a Children's Cinema Club on weekend afternoons. Experimental, lower budget film and video work is shown in the cinematheque. The video library is open from *12.00–17.30 Tue–Sun* for selection and viewing of tapes, for a small extra charge. See the theatre change shape to accommodate its current visual experiment or drama; in the round one day, focused on an endstage the next; sometimes both the action and audience move around. Regular events include lunchtime conversations between writers, artists, critics and the public, and evening talks and seminars on cultural issues.

At the end of the concourse gallery a real live indoor tree marks the entrance to the fully licensed restaurant. This serves hot and cold meals of the wholesome kind *from 12.00–15.00 and 17.00–20.00*. It *closes between 15.00–17.00*, when its tiny annexe opens for tea, coffee and lighter snacks. Centre *open 12.00–23.00 Tue–Sun; closed Mon.*

Oval House

54 Kennington Oval SE11. 01-735 2786. Oval House, whose entrance is directly opposite the entrance to the Oval cricket ground, grew out of a youth club and has been concerned with further education since the mid-70s. That's why so many of its classes and workshops are instant, athletic and with obvious appeal to the young – juggling, mono-cycling, modern dance, music-making. There are also workshops designed to simulate various types of employment, to minimise the shock to the system of going to work for the first time. (In the present economic climate, some have been adapted to deal with signing on for the dole, to minimise the shock of not going to work at all). There are print shop facilities – book on 01-582 7680 and a video project – enquire on 01-582 8374. Children's programmes are arranged in the school holidays. Local children get first go at the booking, via the Borough Play Scheme, but outsiders are welcome.

For adults the two studio theatres, one of them small and the other very small, regularly play host to visiting experimental theatre groups and sometimes present lively productions that have grown out of workshops and classes. Strictly, this is a theatre club, but membership is cheap and immediate.

The small friendly café offers snacks, hot and soft drinks, with two or three hot dishes of the day at lunchtime and in the evening, most with a vegetarian bias. *Open 10.00–22.30 Mon–Sat. Café open 12.30–21.30 Mon–Sun; closed Sat lunch.*

The Place   **3 D 25**

17 Duke's Rd WC1. 01-387 0161. The home base of the
London Contemporary Dance Theatre which presents an
annual season of new and often experimental choreography
in the 250-seat theatre, usually in summer. The home also of
a school for professional dancers whose students give regular
public performances during their three-year full-time course.
When the young professionals point their feet away from the
practice rooms in the evenings and at weekends, classes in
contemporary dance and ballet open for members of the
public – adults at night and children and teenagers on Sat
and Sun.

When the London Contemporary Dance Theatre is on tour
the small theatre is used for a regularly changing programme
of performing arts, the bias not surprisingly towards dance
and movement, but with plenty of scope for visiting fringe
theatre as well. The small bar opens half an hour before
performances and during the intervals. *Open 10.00–22.30
Mon–Sun.*

Riverside Studios

Crisp Rd W6. 01-748 3354. The ex-BBC studios have been
converted into what Irving Whardle of *The Sunday Times*
called 'a powerhouse of the arts'. For audiences there is a
studio theatre which offers a rich mix of drama, dance or
music from Mon–Sat, usually followed by a one-off show or
concert on Sun; and a TV studio where specific BBC
programmes are recorded (tickets available from the BBC in
Portland Place W1). For participators there are regular jazz,
tap and modern dance classes suitable for all levels of ability
(book by the term). There is a bookshop whose stock relates
predominantly, though not exclusively, to the performing
arts and an art gallery whose exhibitions of modern paintings
change monthly.

The huge foyer, with its plentiful tables and chairs and the
changing displays of pictures around its walls, has a bar at
the far end, open during licensing hours, and a long self-
service counter down one wall from which you may buy
snacks, cakes, tea or coffee throughout the day and evening,
seven days a week, and a hot plateful of something
wholesome at lunchtime and before the evening performance. *Open 10.00–23.00 Mon–Sat; 10.30–22.30 Sun. Bookshop and gallery open 12.00–20.00 Tue–Sun.*

BOOKSHOPS

It is not hard to buy books in London – if there is a problem, it is resisting them. Although most areas have their good shops, the best browsing places are Charing Cross Road and Cecil Court, around the British Museum, in Farringdon Road market and in Camden Passage on Thu & Fri. The famous nation-wide high street chain of W.H. Smith, which sells books as well as stationery, toys, records and cassettes, is best for popular titles and paperbacks. Most department stores have book sections and the major art galleries and museums sell specialist publications. For thrift, though with limited choice, keep an eye open for remainder shops and gift books that have proved less popular than their publishers had hoped. What follows here is a selection of the general, the antiquarian and the specialist establishments, all of whom will order books not in stock (subject to availability) and many of whom undertake mail order. Indeed the antiquarian shops, with their appealing catalogues, positively welcome it.

GENERAL

Compendium
234 Camden High St NW1. 01-485 8944. Slightly to the left of general, with politics and SF, alternative technology, feminism, modern poetry and the occult well-represented. The notice boards draw attention to lectures and meetings on radical subjects. *Open 10.00–18.00 Mon–Sat.*

Dillons University Bookshop   **3 F 24**
1 Malet St WC1. 01-636 1577. London's leading academic bookseller, suitably situated in the heart of the London University campus, carries a large general stock. Especially good on political science, history and literature. Don't miss the cheap 'remainders' in the sale room. *Open 09.00–17.30 Mon, Thu & Fri; 10.00–19.30 Tue; 09.00–19.00 Wed; 09.30–13.00 Sat.*

Foyles   **2 H 22**
119 Charing Cross Rd WC2. 01-437 5660. This building houses the largest of them all. Stock is immense and ranges from the latest bestseller to obscure technical tomes. Staff are not noted for their ability to locate specific items, and the new system of grouping books by publisher rather than

author or subject is less than popular. Paying is an interesting ritual – take book to assistant, receive bill, pay at central cashpoint, receive receipt, then retrieve book from assistant in exchange for same. *Open 09.00–18.00 Mon–Sat; until 19.00 Thu.*

Hammicks 6 J 23

1 The Market, Covent Garden WC2. 01-379 6465. Small but intelligently stocked with fiction both modern and classic and a lively range of non-fiction. Particularly good children's department upstairs. *Open 10.00–20.00 Mon–Sat.*

Hatchards 2 I 20

187 Piccadilly W1. 01-439 9921. Old-established (1797), with calm and dignified drawing-room atmosphere. A good stock of books on most subjects, apart from academic or technical. Large paperback section downstairs, excellent children's section upstairs, with rare books beyond it. *Open 09.00– 17.30 Mon–Fri; 09.00–13.00 Sat.*

Hatchards Bookshop in Piccadilly

Mowbrays 2 F 20

28 Margaret St W1. 01–580 2812. Just off Regent Street, a theological bookshop which has expanded to accommodate hardbacks on most subjects, with one entire floor given over to paperbacks. *Open 09.00–17.30 Mon–Fri; Sat Dec only.*

Pan Bookshop   **4 K 6**
154 Fulham Rd SW10. 01-373 4997. Housed in the same
building as the publisher, so if Pan have it in print you'll get
it here. Also other publishers' paperbacks, new hardbacks
(both fiction and non-fiction) and coffee-table books. Note
generous opening hours. *Open 10.00–22.30 Mon–Sat; 14.30–
18.30 Sun.*

Penguin Bookshop   **6 J 23**
Unit 10, The Market, Covent Garden WC2. 01-379 7650. If
by some remote chance a Penguin-in-print is not present it
can be summoned within 24 hours. A whole room of
children's books. Paperbacks from most other publishers,
and some hardbacks too. *Open 10.00–20.00 Mon–Sat.*

John Sandoe   **4 L 11**
10 Blacklands Ter SW3. 01-589 9473. Small but knowledge-
able and extraordinarily well-stocked. Nothing technical,
but the arts and humanities are well represented between
hard and paper covers. *Open 09.30–17.30 Mon–Sat.*

Truslove and Hanson   **2 I 13**
205 Sloane St SW1. 01-235 2128. Especially strong on new
hardback biography, fiction and history with a smart sideline
in personalised stationery. *Open 09.00–17.30 Mon–Fri
(10.00 Wed); 10.00–17.00 Sat.*

ANTIQUARIAN AND SECOND-HAND

Peter Eaton   **1 A 5**
80 Holland Park Av W11. 01-727 5211. Antiquarian and
second-hand hardbacks and out-of-print paperbacks. *Open
10.00–17.00 Mon–Sat.*

G. Heywood Hill   **2 H 17**
10 Curzon St W1. 01-629 0647. A fine literary aura emanates
from the fine bindings, illustrated and colour-plate books.
Nostalgia waits among the children's antique books. *Open
09.00–17.30 Mon–Fri; 09.00–12.30 Sat.*

E. Joseph   **2 F 19**
1 Vere St W1. 01-493 8353. On the third floor above the
Bank of Scotland (ring the bell and travel up in the lift) you
will discover standard sets in leather and cloth, fine bindings,
illustrated books, private press books and a selection of
Victorian and early 20thC watercolour paintings. *Open
09.30–17.30 Mon–Fri.*

Maggs Bros   **2 H 18**

50 Berkeley Sq W1. 01-499 2007. Rare, fine and private press books, early English literature, autographs and manuscripts and Oriental miniatures. *Open 09.30–17.00 Mon–Fri.*

Marlborough Rare Books   **2 I 19**

35 Old Bond St W1. 01-493 6993. There is a small general stock but the specialities are art, architecture and bibliography, each subject with its own catalogue. *Open 09.30– 18.00 Mon–Fri.*

Bernard Quaritch   **2 H 20**

5–8 Lower John St, Golden Sq W1. 01-734 2983. A general stock of lovely rare and antiquarian books, with good sets in travel and natural history, bibliography and pre-20thC English literature. *Open 09.30–17.30 Mon–Fri.*

Bertram Rota   **6 J 23**

30–31 Long Acre WC2. 01-836 0723. A specialist in modern first editions, although most other areas are generously covered as well. *Open 09.30–17.30 Mon–Fri; Sat by appointment only.*

Henry Sotheran   **2 I 20**

2–5 Sackville St W1. 01-734 1150. One of the oldest and most elegant, stocking those books you would expect to find in an old English gentleman's country library – English literature, travel, sporting and natural history books. Also antiquarian prints and maps and new books under the headings of natural history, literature, fine arts and 'books about books'. *Open 09.00–17.30 Mon–Fri.*

SPECIALIST

Arts Council Shop   **6 J 23**

8 Long Acre WC2. 01-836 1359. Not only the Arts Council's own publications but also art books in general, contemporary literature, exhibition catalogues, postcards, posters, prints and clip-frames. *Open 10.00–19.45 Mon–Sat.*

The Book Room, Creative Camera   **3 G 27**

19 Doughty St WC1. 01-405 7562. The front room of this Queen Anne House holds more than 1,000 titles on photography in general and technique for professionals in particular. Elsewhere in the house Coo Press publishes books and magazines on the subject of pigeons (fancy!) and the monthly journal *Creative Camera*. *Open 10.00–18.00 Mon–Fri. Sat by appointment only.*

Louis Bondy   3 H 24
16 Little Russell St WC1. 01-405 2733. Antiquarian bookseller who knows that small is beautiful. Huge collection of miniature books presided over by a world authority, who is also the author of a book on the subject. *Open 10.30–18.30 Mon–Fri; 10.30–17.15 Sat.*

Cinema Bookshop   3 H 24
13–14 Gt Russell St WC1. 01-637 0206. Mecca for movie buffs. Books on every aspect of the cinema, including out-of-prints, together with stills, posters and magazines. *Open 10.30–17.30 Mon–Sat.*

Collets Chinese Gallery and Bookshop   3 H 24
40 Gt Russell St WC1. 01-580 7538. Books in Chinese and books about China, and all you've ever wanted to know about acupuncture. Chinese artefacts and antiques. *Open 10.00–18.00 Mon–Sat.*

Collets International Bookshop   2 I 22
129–131 Charing Cross Rd WC2. 01-734 0782. Actually a general bookshop, but with a strong speciality in Russian and Slavonic studies. Classical records, too. *Open 09.30–20.00 Mon–Fri; 09.30–18.00 Sat.*

Dance Books   5 J 22
9 Cecil Ct WC2. 01-836 2314. Anything published in Britain (and many things published in the US) on any aspect of dance and movement find their way here to join the 50-odd titles published in-house, the prints, posters, records and sheet music for classes, and the dance-related ephemera. *Open 11.00–19.00 Mon–Sat.*

Forbidden Planet   3 H 23
23 Denmark St WC2. 01-836 4179. Specialists in unreal worlds with a fantastic array of science fiction comics and paperbacks, including US imports. Also at 58 St Giles High St WC2. 01-379 6042. Here you will find books and magazines on films and TV programmes, SF and other. *Open 10.00–18.00 Mon–Sat (19.00 Thu).*

French's Theatre Bookshop   2 E 22
52–56 Fitzroy St W1. 01-387 9373. Samuel French publish playscripts. Their shop aims for a total coverage of the legitimate theatre scene – not only scripts but books on every aspect of drama, stage design, voice, lighting, make-up and volumes of theatrical criticism. *Open 09.30–17.30 Mon–Fri.*

Geographia 6 K 27

63 Fleet St EC4. 01-353 2701. The retail outlet of Geographia and Robert Nicholson Publications where you will find this guide and its companion London titles, as well as maps, plans and guides covering the rest of Britain and much of the world. *Open 09.00–17.25 Mon–Fri.*

Hachette 2 H 20

4 Regent Place (off Regent St) W1. 01-734 5259. Books in French and books about France, mostly paperbacks. Strong on novels, politics and travel. *Open 09.30–18.00 Mon–Fri; 09.30–13.00 Sat.*

HMSO Bookshop 3 I 23

49 High Holborn WC1. 01-928 6977. The retail outlet for the publications of Her Majesty's Stationery Office, which also carries parliamentary publications from overseas (EEC, UN and others), the full range of Ordnance Survey maps, Ancient Monuments Publications and regional guides. *Open 08.30–17.00 Mon–Fri.*

London Art Bookshop 1 D 7

7 Holland St W8. 01-937 6996. Comprehensive international stock of books on art and architecture, photography and design. *Open 09.30–18.00 Mon–Sat.*

Arthur Probsthain & Co 3 H 23

41 Gt Russell St WC1. 01-636 1096. Specialists in the Orient and Africa with new and second-hand books on the language, history, politics, art and archaeology of those areas. *Open 10.00–17.30 Mon–Fri; 11.00–15.30 Sat.*

Robinson and Watkins 5 J 22

19–21 Cecil Ct WC2. 01-836 3778. Continues to supply ancient and modern, new and second-hand volumes on mysticism, religion, the occult and alternative culture. The incense of the 60s still lingers. *Open 10.00–18.00 Tue–Sat. Closed Mon.*

St George's Gallery 5 J 19

8 Duke St SW1. 01-930 0935. Books on the fine and decorative arts, mostly new with a few second-hand. Also beautifully illustrated foreign exhibition catalogues. *Open 10.00–18.00 Mon–Fri; 10.00–13.00 Sat.*

Stanford 6 J 23

12 Long Acre WC2. 01-836 1321. Find your way to this most comprehensive map shop in the world and you need never be lost again – British maps, European survey maps, coastal,

aeronautical, and geological charts, flat and folded maps of most countries, globes, street plans and guide books. *Open 09.00–17.00 Mon–Fri; 10.00–14.00 Sat.*

Travis and Emery   5 J 22
17 Cecil Ct WC2. 01-240 2129. A cloud of musical and theatrical ephemera with a rich core of new and second-hand books on music, and a small but beautifully stocked antiquarian section. Second-hand and antiquarian printed music. *Open 10.00–18.00 Mon–Fri; 10.00–13.00 Sat.*

A. Zwemmer   2 I 22
Litchfield St WC2. 01-836 4710. The visual arts – film, art, architecture and design – in a vast range of new, second-hand and antiquarian books, with a special area for cut-price remainders. *Open 09.30–17.30 Mon–Fri; 09.30–16.00 Sat.*

CINEMAS

The great age of cinema building was from 1910 to the mid 1930s. The structures that went up richly deserved their title of picture palaces with their panelling and gilt, velvet seating and glittering chandeliers, deep carpets, domes and painted ceilings. By contrast, the small local cinemas that followed were aptly known as flea pits. But even here the glamorous appeal of the new movies was such that the more serious members of the community feared for the future of church, novel and even family.

The Second World War and the invention of television each hit the cinema in its own way and there was anxiety about its survival. A significant number of buildings were converted to bingo halls. But the idea of adapting a large picture house into a complex of two, three or even four small cinemas reclaimed economic viability.

Today the cinema flourishes in various styles. You can watch popular films on general release in one of the large picture houses around Leicester Square or, more cheaply, at a smaller local or multi-screen cinema; and foreign, experimental and classic films get an airing in the many specialist cinemas. *Time Out*, *City Limits* and *The Standard* list what's on, where and when. (And don't forget to check on the Arts Centres cinemas, especially the Barbican and the progressive ICA.)

WEST END CINEMAS

ABC 1 & 2, 135 Shaftesbury Av WC2. 01-836 8861.
Biograph, 47 Wilton Rd SW1. 01-834 1624. Britain's oldest.
Cinecenta 1, 2, 3 & 4, Panton St W1. 01-930 0631.
Classic, Oxford St W1. 01-636 0310.
Classic Cinema Complex, Haymarket SW1. 01-839 1527.
Classic, 93 Shaftesbury Av WC1. 01-734 5414.
Dominion, Tottenham Court Rd W1. 01-580 9562.
Empire 1 & 2, Leicester Sq WC2. 01-437 1234.
Film Centa, Charing Cross Rd WC2. 01-437 4815.
Leicester Square Theatre, Leicester Sq WC2. 01-930 5252.
Odeon, Haymarket SW1. 01-930 2738/2771.
Odeon, Kensington High St W8. 01-602 6644.
Odeon, Leicester Sq WC2. 01-930 6111.
Odeon, Marble Arch W2. 01-723 2011.
Plaza 1, 2, 3 & 4, Lower Regent St W1. 01-437 1234.
Prince Charles, Leicester Pl, Leicester Sq WC2. 01-437 8181.
Scene 1, 2, 3 & 4, Swiss Centre, Leicester Sq WC2. 01-439 4446.
Times Centa, Baker St Station NW1. 01-935 9772.
Warner West End, Leicester Sq WC2 01-439 0791.

SPECIALIST CINEMAS

Academy 1, 2 & 3   **2 G 21**
165 Oxford St W1. ONE 01-437 2981. TWO 01-437 5129.
THREE 01-437 8819. Three-screen cinema showing the
latest continental and festival successes with occasional
revivals. If you need food for the body as well as the mind it
has its own restaurant, Vasco & Piero's Pavilion (book on
01-437 8774) accessible from the cinema or from its own
entrance in Poland Street. Traditional Italian meals served
daily (*closed Sat lunch & all Sun*).

Classic, Hampstead
Pond St, Hampstead NW3. 01-794 4000. A three-screen
local showing current releases but with double-feature
classic revivals for insomniacs at *23.00 Fri & Sat.*

Classic Leicester Square   **2 I 22**
35–37 Charing Cross Rd WC2. 01-930 6915. Keeps its
projectors whirring *all night, every night*. The films are
international, often sensational, sometimes obscure.

Curzon   **2 I 17**
Curzon St W1. 01-499 3737. Deliciously comfortable sur-

roundings in which to watch quality new releases. It's wise to book. Good coffee on sale in the foyer.

Electric Screen   1 A 8
191 Portobello Rd W11. 01-727 4992. Of interest in itself as one of the oldest purpose-built cinemas in London. Offers an esoteric mix of first-releases, including underground and continental films and revivals of rare and otherwise elusive ones. Membership at the door.

Everyman
Holly Bush Vale, Hampstead NW3. 01-435 1525. Imaginative programmes of continental classics and British and American revivals – most of the films for one performance only, so don't hang about.

Gala Royal   2 D 16
Edgware Rd W2. 01-262 2345. Specialises in Arabic films, some of them subtitled.

Gate at Notting Hill   1 A 8
Notting Hill Gate W11. 01-727 5750. 'Quality art films' are what they offer here, frequently of foreign origin, and the choice is adventurous and interesting. *Late shows every night*. Membership at door.

Gate Bloomsbury   3 F 26
Brunswick Sq WC1. 01-837 8402. A two-screen cinema in the Brunswick Estate (notice the appealing design which makes the flats look rather like a series of conservatories sliding down a slope). There's a shop for relevant posters and books, a licensed bar, and the distinctive Gate flavour in the film selection. *Late shows Fri & Sat*. Membership at door.

Gate Mayfair   2 I 18
Mayfair Hotel, Stratton St W1. 01-493 2031. Miniature cinema within a well-appointed hotel, which means you have ready access, before or after the performance, to the restaurant, coffee shop, bar or Aloha cocktail bar with its simulated Polynesian weather and resident crocodile. Membership at door.

Lumiere   5 J 22
St Martin's La WC2. 01-836 0691. Smart, modern cinema (formerly The Lane) showing quality films – sometimes political, usually foreign and subtitled.

Minema 2 I 14

New Berkeley Hotel, 45 Knightsbridge SW7. 01-235 4225. Truly minimal in size but with maximum comfort. Programmes of modern classics, only interrupted if it has been hired for private showing.

National Film Theatre 6 M 24

South Bank SE1. 01-928 3232. The two cinemas and bookshop are really for serious students of movie history but the rare foreign films, classic revivals and seasons specialising in the work of one director or one star are also extremely popular with those audiences whose approach is more hedonistic. It is a club, and children have their own membership and their own weekend programmes. The licensed buffet, open daily, has a nice line in snacks.

Roxie Cinema Club 2 I 21

76 Wardour St W1. 01-439 3657. By day a small preview cinema used by the movie companies in Wardour Street to check rushes or introduce press and distributors to finished copies. *In the evenings, and weekend afternoons*, it offers a catholic selection of films in repertory – classic revivals, rock movies, the occasional arty foreign number. No membership required these days.

Scala

275–277 Pentonville Rd N1. 01-278 8052. Worth the trek to enjoy the ever-changing repertory of double bills to suit brows of every possible height – trash and blockbusters, art films, blue movies, grue movies and classics of all nationalities – frequently shown *late-night, or even all night*. Licensed café within. Membership at door.

Screen-on-the-Green 3 E 22

Islington Green, Upper St N1. 01-226 3520. New films, usually, with occasional revivals. *Late shows on Fri & Sat*. Membership at the door.

Screen-on-the-Hill

203 Haverstock Hill NW3. 01-435 3366. Good, new films that are not going to turn up elsewhere, and revivals of same. Membership at the door.

Studio 1, 2 and 3 2 G 20

225 Oxford St W1. 01-437 3300. Three screens which offer a mixture of current releases, recent revivals and foreign films.

FAMOUS HOUSES AND PALACES ────────

Since 1866 the round blue plaque has been a familiar sight on the walls of London buildings, indicating an association with an architect, artist, composer, politician, scientist, soldier or writer of note. But all that the visitor can do is stare and marvel. However, just a few such houses have been preserved as a kind of shrine and opened to the public for closer scrutiny. A selection of these is detailed here, in the company of several unique houses famous in themselves for the quality of their architecture and furnishings, and of three royal palaces, each maintained as a combination of museum and art gallery and as intriguing for present content as for past illustrious occupants.

Apsley House   **2 I 16**
149 Piccadilly W1. 01-499 5676. An Adam house, altered in the early 19thC by Wyatt (who added the portico and the Bath stone facing) known as No 1 London when it was the home of the first Duke of Wellington. Now administered by the Victoria and Albert Museum and a perfect setting for the Iron Duke's silver, plate, porcelain and priceless paintings. Buy your ticket from the bookstall in the entrance hall. Turn first left into the old muniment room to be dazzled by displays of plate and china, the Empress Josephine's Egyptian table-centre in biscuit porcelain, its obelisks and sphinxes the colour of icing sugar, and the first Duke's medals.
Right from the entrance hall is the inner hall, lined with busts, from whose east side stairs descend past a portrait of the seventh Duke, who presented the house to the nation, to subterranean corridors lined with maps, pictures, caricatures and the doors to the Ladies and Gents.
To the north of the inner hall a graceful stairway leads up, past an unexpectedly colossal marble statue of Napoleon, to the first floor. This you can circle through elegant interconnecting rooms with massive candelabra (electric now). Beneath ornate white and gold ceilings, and between long windows giving on to Hyde Park and the Wellington Arch, hangs a rich collection of paintings, among them works by Velasquez, Rubens and Murillo. Don't miss the covered watercolours, on music stands, which show each room as it was. You can't miss the centrepiece on the dining table, a

gift in 1816 from the then Prince Regent of Portugal; the nymphs and griffins seem set to knock the eye out of anyone reaching for the salt in a hurry.

Open 10.00–18.00 Tue–Thu & Sat; 14.30–18.00 Sun. Closed Nat Hols. Charge.

Banqueting House   **5 L 21**

Whitehall SW1. 01-930 4179. A splendid survivor of the royal palace of Whitehall, the principal London residence of the Court during the reign of Henry VIII, which was rebuilt during the reigns of Elizabeth I and James I. The present hall, by Inigo Jones, was built in 1625, and was the first Palladian building to be completed in England. When it is not in use for government functions, you may ascend to the gracious and spacious banqueting hall itself and admire the nine allegorical ceiling paintings, designed for Charles I by Peter Paul Rubens. His reward on their completion in 1635 included a knighthood. The central oval shows the *Apotheosis of James I*, and the picture to the north of the hall the birth and coronation of Charles himself.

There are two other claims to fame, which have almost achieved the status of legend. One is the weathercock which James II is reputed to have had set up to indicate whether or not the wind was likely to blow the Prince of Orange across the seas in his direction. The other is the tablet which marks the window through which Charles I stepped to his execution. (If you call on the morning of 30th January you will find the hall has become a Chapel for the sake of a service in honour of the King.)

Open 10.00–17.00 Tue–Sat; 14.00–17.00 Sun. Closed Mon, (except Nat Hols) and when in use. Charge.

Carlyle's House   **4 M 8**

24 Cheyne Row SW3. 01-352 7087. Thomas Carlyle, the formidable 'sage of Chelsea', lived here with his wife Jane from 1834 until their respective deaths. The modest 18thC house has been preserved as nearly as possible as it was in their day, and so successfully that there is an eerie sense of their immanence. Especially as Carlyle's hat still hangs inside the door.

In the parlour, where you will be asked to sign the visitor's book with the quill provided, notice Robert Tait's painting *A Chelsea Interior* which shows the room as it is now but with its remarkable owners in their places. The back dining room, where they breakfasted, and the china closet, off it, are full of pictures and personal possessions. Go through to the back door for a glimpse of the garden (best seen from upstairs) and follow the stairs down to look into the crude basement kitchens. Upstairs is the library, or drawing room, in which Carlyle wrote *The French Revolution* – and in which he heard the news that the first half of the manuscript had accidentally been burned as rubbish. (Whereupon he wrote it again). Next door is Mrs Carlyle's bedroom and adjoining dressing room, its washstand set with fresh towels as if a guest is expected.

The second floor, once Carlyle's bedroom, is now the caretaker's flat, but you may visit the strange sky-lit attic study above it, built as a haven from distracting sounds but a total failure since it had the curious effect of magnifying them. Here are his desk and, in show cases, his books, manuscripts and letters – with bound volumes of facsimile letters waiting to be opened on the table.

Open 11.00–17.00 Wed–Sat; 14.00–17.00 Sun. Closed Mon, Tue & Nov–Mar. Charge.

Chiswick House

Burlington La W4. 01-995 0508. A lovely Palladian villa, created 1725–9 by the third Earl of Burlington, architect and patron of the arts. His is the exterior. The interior and gardens are by Kent. His Lordship's actual residence was a nearby Jacobean mansion, now demolished. This house was designed as a gallery where fine pictures were hung and artists and writers entertained. For the best effect approach from Burlington Lane Gate (just on the Great Chertsey Road) and pass through the courtyard lined with neo-classical busts. The ticket desk is immediately behind the small door beneath the main portico. Go straight on into the *octagon hall* from which three doors lead – ahead into what was the library, right to the south lobby and left to the north lobby. These rooms house an exhibition on the development of the house and gardens. Behind the desk, stairs spiral up to the almost Baroque splendour of the first floor.

Here the centrepiece is the octagonal *domed salon*, hung with massive historical and allegorical pictures and with classical busts (not the originals) between the doorways. The inside of the dome is painted in perspective to make it appear higher, a trick Kent had already used in the cupola room at Kensington Palace. The surrounding rooms don't all lead out of each other, so a certain amount of confusion is inevitable.

Start with the *red velvet room* (named for its wall covering,

Chiswick House

now replaced by flock in the appropriate colour). Here are
two pictures by Sebastiano Ricci and an elaborate Kent
ceiling. From here go into the *blue velvet room* with portraits
of Inigo Jones and Pope and an immensely busy ceiling
surrounding a central figure of Architecture. It opens on to
the *red closet* with its demure panelled ceiling. Go back
through blue and red rooms to the *gallery* where everything,
including the statues in the niches, has been scaled down to
make the whole seem larger. Next, into the *green velvet
room* with its gilded ceiling and pictures by Ricci. Beyond is
the so-called *bedchamber* and small *dressing room*. Return
through *green velvet room* and *domed salon* to the stairs.

The gardens, open to the public, are quite beautiful, with
wooded areas, a canal abob with waterfowl, an orangery and
an Italian garden. To the right of the house a lane leads to
the cafeteria (*11.00–16.00 Tue–Fri; 11.00–18.00 Sat & Sun*)
and public lavatories.

*Open 09.30–13.00; 14.00–16.00 Tue–Sun, Oct–Mar (to 18.30
Mar–Oct). Closed Mon, Tue in Oct–Mar. Charge.*

Dickens' House   3 G 27
48 Doughty St W1. 01-405 2127. Charles Dickens lived and
worked here from April 1837 until December 1839 – not

much more than two and a half years – yet in that relatively short time he finished the last five chapters of *Pickwick Papers*, most of *Oliver Twist*, 20 monthly instalments of *Nicholas Nickleby* and the first few pages of *Barnaby Rudge*, and established his reputation as a writer. Here, too, his beloved sister-in-law Mary Hogarth died at the age of 17, an event which affected the rest of his life and is said to have inspired the death scene of Little Nell. The house is cared for by the Dickens Fellowship – who publish *The Dickensian* three times a year – and is packed with memorabilia.

Among numerous fascinating exhibits – many presented by the Comte de Suzannet and his wife – are the Dickens family tree; his desk, chair and the china monkey without which he couldn't start work; playbills and manuscript pages; a copy of *David Copperfield* which went to the Antarctic with Scott and is stained with seal oil to prove it; letters and portraits; Dickens' own annotated reading copies which he used in amateur theatricals; and framed sketches of some of his unforgettable characters, including Mr Micawber, Nicholas Nickleby, Barnaby Rudge with Grip, Dombey and Son and Little Nell. The Dickens House Library, an amalgamation of the collections of F.G. Kitton and B.W. Matz, is accessible to students of his work, but please make an appointment. *Open 10.00–17.00 Mon–Sat. Closed Sun & Nat Hols. Charge.*

Fenton House

Hampstead Gro NW3. 01-435 3471. Built c1693, its early history is unknown. It was bought by a merchant called Philip Fenton in 1793 and slightly altered by his son, c1807. Though it passed through other hands, it kept the name of Fenton, and was bequeathed to the National Trust in 1952 by Lady Binning, its late owner, together with her pictures, furniture and porcelain. Today the chief of its many charms is that it houses the Benton Fletcher collection of musical instruments, most of them in such good working order that, if you are lucky, you can tour the house to a background of harpsichord or virginal.

On the ground floor, the *dining room* has a collection of 11 pictures by Sir William Nicholson and a harpsichord by Burket Shudi and Broadwood. The *porcelain room* has English porcelain from Chelsea, Bow and Worcester in its left alcove and continental porcelain from Meissen, Nymphenburg and Zurich in its right. The 17thC harpshichord belongs to the Queen. The *oriental room* has porcelain from

the Sung, Ming and Ching Dynasties. On the staircase hangs
William IV by Lawrence.

On the first floor the *Rockingham room* has a large
collection of that pottery, a Burket Shudi harpsichord and a
16thC Italian spinet. The collection in the *blue porcelain
room* is Chinese 17th and 18thC. The 18thC harpsichord is
by the Kirckmans, the 17thC Italian virginal by Baffo. The
drawing room, with its elegant satinwood furniture, has
beautiful Worcester and Meissen porcelain. The *pink room*
has 17thC needlework pictures, Staffordshire figures and an
early 18thC spinet.

The *attic floor's* six small rooms contain the bulk of the
instrument collection – among them harpsichords,
clavichords, a rectangular 18thC piano, grand pianos and
virginals. And don't neglect to stare out of the windows – the
views of Hampstead and parts of London are stunning.

*Open 11.00–17.00 Mon–Wed, Sat & Nat Hols; 14.00–17.00
Sun, Apr–Oct. 11.00–17.00 Sat, 14.00–17.00 Sun in Nov,
Feb & Mar. Closed Dec & Jan. Charge.*

Ham House

Richmond, Surrey. 01-940 1950. A richly Baroque Stuart
house on the banks of the Thames outside Richmond, now
administered by the V & A and offering the best glimpse of
17thC life you will get anywhere in England. Built in 1610, it
belonged to the first Earl of Dysart until 1639 when his
daughter Elizabeth and her husband the Duke of Lauderdale took it on, decorated it in the opulent style preserved
today and furnished it with rare and beautiful items.

Enter by the ***great hall*** under the gaze of Dysart portraits and
buy tickets and postcards just inside. Through the door in
the right hand corner of the hall you will find the ***gentleman's
parlour*** with its 20-minute audio-visual show, recommended
for openers but equally fascinating after a tour of the rooms.
Just beyond the parlour is a display of photographs and
drawings of changes made to the house over the years, and
stairs down to the basement. Here are the servant's hall,
domestic utensils, and the National Trust shop selling
Nature neatly packaged in sachet and jar. The tour proper
begins in the

Marble dining room, straight ahead through the great hall.
18thC parquet replaces the original marble floor but the gilt-
leather wall hangings are original. At first, the Duke's apartments were to the right, the Duchess's to the left, but a swap-
ping of rooms has mixed up their titles. Go right into the

Duke's dressing room, with floral marquetry cabinet, and ebonised table and candlestands of 1670. Continue through to the

Duchess's bedchamber. The feathered bed is a reconstruction, the Duchess's box and brass-bound jewel case are original, the ceiling painting over the bed is in the style of Verrio.

Duke's closet. The most remarkable item is the 17thC writing cabinet. Retrace your steps through the marble dining room to the

Withdrawing room. Oriental lacquer pier glass and table of 1675 and ebonised and gilded armchairs of 1680. Next the

Yellow bedchamber. The bed hangings are modern but the cabinet is of the 1630s and the porcelain is Chinese, K'ang Hsi period.

White closet. Note the bust of the Duchess's mother over the chimney and the painting of Ham House from the South over the fireplace.

Duchess's private closet. Richly decorated with reproduction hangings and original furniture. An unprepossessing passage returns you to the great hall and from there to the private chapel, on the other side, and the inner hall with its 18thC harpsichord and massive paintings. From here rises the sumptuous great staircase, leading to the state apartments above. At the top turn left into the

Yellow satin room, its curtains drawn to protect the 17thC Flemish tapestries, after paintings by Poussin.

The yellow satin dressing room, off it, is used to display 18thC furniture and family portraits. Cross the landing to the

Museum room with its textile collection and faded Lyons brocaded silk toilet set admiring itself in a mirror stained with age. Next door is the

Cabinet of miniatures – tiny portraits and a lock of hair from the executed Essex, favourite of Elizabeth I. Cross the

Round gallery, with its family portraits, including some by Lely and Kneller, to the luscious

North drawing room with its 17th or early 18thC tapestries of rustic pursuits and its unusual twisted half columns beside the mantelpiece. Off it is the beautiful little

Green closet, its ceiling papered with tempera paintings by Franz Cleyn. The north drawing room opens onto the

Long gallery, where 22 family portraits seem to wince at the sound of alien shoes on the parquet. At the far end turn right to the

Library closet and library, both added to the house by the

Duke and Duchess of Lauderdale. The small but valuable collection was sold in the 1930s. Return to the long gallery and take the opposite door to the

Ante chamber to the Queen's bedchamber. The wall hangings were once blue, but after 300 years they had a right to fade. Continue to the

Queen's bedchamber with its view of the gardens and avenue. Originally prepared for Catherine of Braganza though somewhat altered since. The tapestries are mid 18thC, hung when the room was converted into a drawing room. Next to it the

Queen's closet is a most private inner sanctum, containing a rare 17thC slope-backed sleeping chair. Retrace your steps to the long gallery and through the north drawing room and round gallery to the great staircase and the way out. (Yes, there are a number of rooms not open to the public, and yes there is at least one secret passage.)

The formal gardens are well worth a wander and in the old kitchen garden, now given over to roses, you will find the orangery, part of which is now a tearoom with tables on the lawn. The public lavatories are in the stable yard, between house and orangery.

Open 14.00–18.00 Tue–Sun, Apr–Sep; 12.00–16.00 Tue–Sun, Oct–Mar. Closed mornings, Mon & Nat Hols. Charge.

Hampton Court Palace

Hampton Ct Middx. 01-977 8441. Begun by Cardinal Wolsey in 1514 and given to Henry VIII in 1529 in an unsuccessful attempt to regain favour. Enlarged by Henry VIII, repaired by Charles II, extended by Christopher Wren under William and Mary, with further interior decoration carried out on the orders of Queen Anne, George I and George II. The state apartments were first opened to the public by Queen Victoria. It is vast, grand, on a prime riverside site, with a collection of Italian masterpieces among other important paintings (though these are sometimes on loan to other exhibitions) and its grounds, which include the famous *Maze*, are sweeping, varied and beautiful.

Enter through the west front and you are in the Base Court with ticket office and lavatories at one corner. Continue through to Clock Court, named for Nicholas Oursian's wondrous astronomical clock. Opening off this are the book and souvenir shop, a small exhibition on the construction and function of the palace (which helps put it into perspective) and the entrance to the state apartments.

King's staircase. In your amazement at the abundant wall and ceiling painting by Antonio Verrio don't ignore the delicate wrought iron balustrade by Tijou.

King's guard chamber. Where the Yeoman guarded William III. Their weaponry is arranged above the wall panelling in an arresting design by the King's gunsmith. From here you proceed around the outer and inner rooms, with views of the grounds from the windows of the former.

King's first presence chamber. The first of the Wren rooms. Dominated by Kneller's magnificent equestrian portrait of William III.

Second presence chamber. With two Tintorettos and three Rousseaus among its pictures.

King's audience chamber. Here are the *Nine Muses* by Tintoretto and the *Marriage of St Catherine* by Veronese.

King's drawing room. The elaborate overmantel is by Grinling Gibbons.

King William III's state bedchamber. The ceiling is by Verrio, the portrait over the mantel by Lely, the flower paintings over the doors by Bogdani.

King's dressing room. Or little bedchamber, with a ceiling by Verrio.

King's writing closet. Look in the mirror above the fireplace to see all the preceding rooms reflected back.

Queen Mary's closet. She never used it but it was once hung with embroideries stitched by her and her ladies.

Queen's gallery. A Grinling Gibbons cornice and Gobelins tapestries of the history of Alexander the Great. The imposing blue and white vases with the little hollow excrescenses were designed to hold tulips and hyacinths.

Queen's bedchamber. The crimson damask upholstery on the bed is original, the ceiling by Thornhill.

Queen's drawing room. Wall and ceiling paintings by Verrio. Look through the windows for a perfect view of a formal Baroque garden, its three radiating avenues intersected by a huge half-moon of trees and water.

Queen's audience chamber. The tapestry is 16thC Flemish.

Public dining room. Decorated by Vanbrugh with a cornice by Grinling Gibbons and an unusual *Adoration of the Magi* by Sebastiano Ricci.

Prince of Wales suite. The tapestry in the drawing room is one of a 17thC set of *Acts of the Apostles.* The sumptuous bed, with embroidered silk hangings, was made for Queen Charlotte in 1775–8.

Prince of Wales staircase. Reached through a series of more discreet royal chambers, including Queen Caroline's private chapel and bathing closet.

Cartoon gallery. The tapestries were copied from Raphael cartoons, now in the Victoria and Albert Museum, for which the gallery was designed.

Communication gallery. Between the King's and Queen's state apartments. Hung with portraits of the 'Windsor Beauties' of the court of Charles II by Lely.

Wolsey's closet. The only remaining room with the full flavour of the original palace.

Cumberland suite. Designed by Kent and named for 'Butcher' Cumberland of Culloden who lived in it for a time.

Queen's staircase. Its balustrade by Tijou.

Queen's guard chamber. Hung with Kneller portraits.

Queen's presence chamber. Designed by Vanbrugh.

Haunted gallery. Return to Queen's staircase and enter the gallery, moving from the 'new' Wren building into the Tudor one. The haunting is by Catherine Howard.

Chapel Royal. The stunning vaulted ceiling with gilded pendants, the wall paintings and trompe l'oeil window by Thornhill, and the elaborate oak reredos by Grinling Gibbons can all be viewed from the privileged position of the Royal pew.

Great watching chamber. Continue along the haunted gallery to this hugely impressive Tudor room, hung with Flemish tapestries, the daylight filtered through 19thC stained glass.

Horn room. A serving room, with steps down to the kitchens.

Great Hall. A truly grand finale to the tour, built in the 1530s with a superb hammerbeam roof and a dais at one end for the high table. Originally there was an open hearth and vents in the roof for the smoke.

Wolsey rooms and Renaissance picture gallery. The Wolsey rooms are discovered through the King's guard chamber. A lobby links them with a corner of Base Court from which the Renaissance gallery, with its fine display of pictures painted on wood, can be reached.

Kitchens. Those interested in the practicalities of running such a magnificent palace should return to the north east corner of Base Court to inspect the *buttery*, *wine cellar* and *great kitchens*.

North of the palace, and between it and the *Maze*, you will find a licensed restaurant, a large cafeteria and a summer ice cream stall.

Open 09.30–18.00 Mon–Sun Apr–Sept; to 17.00 Oct–Mar. Closed winter Nat Hols. Charge.

Hogarth's House

Hogarth La, Great West Rd W4. 01-994 6757. Ignore if you can the undistinguished surrounding buildings and the thundering traffic on the Great West Road and remember that this was William Hogarth's country house from 1749 until the night before he died 15 years later. There is little furniture and no attempt to set the interior as it was in his day. But an unrivalled collection of prints, 'visual writings' satirising the life of his day, press around the walls of the small rooms.

Turn right through the front door to the servants' hall for booklets and postcards. Pass through into the kitchen site for the *Harlot's Progress*, the *Election* prints and *Marriage à la Mode*. (If the curator has time, he will 'read' one to you, showing it to be as vivid as the best bed-time story.) Left across the hall in the dining room don't miss jolly *Beer Street* and dismal *Gin Lane*. Upstairs, turn right into Hogarth's bedroom where hangs the *Stage Coach*, depicting the long-lost Angel at Islington, and an original copper plate for the illustrations of Samuel Butler's poem *Hudibras*. Look respectfully down into the garden at the mulberry tree, survivor of 18thC lightning and 20thC bombing.

Left is the best parlour, with a beautifully sculptural fragment of the aforementioned mulberry and a facsimile of Hogarth's *Self-portrait with Pug*. Pass through into the library for the first plate Hogarth created to please himself – the *Taste of the Times* – full of characteristic prejudice against those who preferred Italian opera and other foreign entertainments to the home-grown talents of Shakespeare and his countrymen.

Open 11.00–18.00 Mon–Sat; 14.00–18.00 Sun. Closed Tue, winter Nat Hols, and at 16.00 Oct–Mar. Free.

Dr Johnson's House   6 K 27

17 Gough Sq, off Fleet St EC4. 01-353 3745. He lived here from 1748–1759 and it was in the attic that much of the famous *Dictionary* was compiled, with the help of six copyists. It is the only one of his London homes to be definitely identified (and if you think it hard to find console yourself that the great Carlyle, seeking it out in 1832, recorded the same problem in his diary.)

Ring the bell for admission and buy a ticket in the front hall. Each room is furnished with such detailed handboards, identifying the many paintings, letters and effects, that the guidebook is only necessary as a souvenir.

In the *dining room* note especially the first edition of the *Dictionary* and the oil by E.M. Ward of Dr J reading the manuscript of Oliver Goldsmith's *Vicar of Wakefield*. In the *parlour* – portraits of Johnson, Boswell, Sheridan, Reynolds and David Garrick. Go up the creaking stairs to the landing, with its pictures of the houses in which he lived and died. Off it lie the *drawing room* – more portraits and personal effects – and *Miss Williams' room* with Hayman's painting of Wesley preaching to a congregation which includes Johnson. Up again to the next landing with its stone from the Great Wall of China. Off it the *library*, possibly the Doctor's bedroom, with books, letters and playbills. Next to it, the *will room* (the will is covered with a blind which you are invited to raise) and James E. Doyle's painting of a literary party at Sir Joshua Reynolds' with Johnson, Boswell and other famous guests. Up again to the *garret*, restored after bomb damage and said to be much as it was when the huge work was in progress, though without the copyists' tables which made Boswell liken it to a 'counting house'.
Open 11.00–17.30 Mon–Sat, May–Sep; 11.00–17.00 Mon–Sat, Oct to Apr. Closed Sun & Nat Hols. Charge.

Keats' House

Wentworth Pl, Keats Gro NW3. 01-435 2062. The house is actually a pair of semi-detached houses, built by Dilke and Charles Armitage Brown in 1815–16, with a pleasant shared garden. Later the Brawne family took over Dilke's house and Keats shared Brown's for much of his most prolific period, 1818–21. This is where he wrote, among many others, *To the Nightingale* (under a plum tree in the garden, which has since been replaced), *Lamia*, *La Belle Dame Sans Merci* and *On a Grecian Urn*, and where he became engaged to Fanny Brawne. For such a short life there is a wealth of memorabilia, much of it displayed in the rooms of the house which, although it has now been knocked into one, is believed still to have much the same appearance as it had in his day.

As you enter, *Mrs Brawne's rooms* are to the right – with guide books and information in the front one – *Brown's sitting room* is the front room to the left and *Keats' sitting room* is immediately behind it. Beyond these is *Miss Chester's drawing room* and pretty conservatory, added in 1839, but as full of letters, pictures and annotated books as the rest of the house. Stairs lead down to the basement where you can see the kitchens and cellars of both houses.

Interior of Keats' House

Upstairs, Keats' and Brown's bedrooms are accessible, while the Brawne rooms are given over to the Keats Memorial Library, available for the use of serious students, not only of Keats himself, but also of Byron, Coleridge, Lamb, Leigh Hunt, Shelley and Wordsworth (by appointment only).
Open 10.00–13.00 & 14.00–18.00 Mon–Sat; 14.00–17.00 Sun. Free.

Kensington Palace 1 D 9
Kensington Gdns W8. 01-937 9561. The former Nottingham House was rebuilt by Wren for William III and extended and redecorated by Williams Benson and Kent for George I. It was the principal residence of the sovereign until the death of George II in 1760. Queen Victoria and George V's Queen, Mary, were both born here and the private apartments are still used by members of the royal family, among them Princess Margaret and the Prince and Princess of

Wales. Standing to one side of the lovely Kensington Gardens, it remains one of the most charming and least awe-inspiring of palaces. Even the sumptuous state apartments, the only part open to the public, seem compact and accessible.

Buy tickets, guide books and cards inside the small entrance and ascend the *Queen's staircase* into the Queen's apartments, which traditionally lie to the left of the state entrance with the King's apartments to the right. *The Queen's gallery*, designed by Wren and with Kneller's *Peter the Great* and Lely's *Duchess of York* among its portraits, leads to the *Queen's closet* where Anne had her final quarrel with Sarah, Duchess of Marlborough. Beyond is the *Queen's dining room*, with its original panelling, and the *Queen's drawing room*, both used by Queen Mary II. Right out of the drawing room, the *Queen's bedchamber* is so dimly lit it's very tempting to creep into the state fourposter, used by James I, and go to sleep.

Ahead, the rooms become larger and more royal. First the *privy chamber*, its ceiling by Kent, its tapestries from Mortlake, its window with a view of Princess Margaret's house. Next the imposing *presence chamber* with another Kent ceiling, but this time with 'arabesque decoration in the Pompeiian manner', the first of its kind in England. Beyond is the *King's grand staircase*, its balustrades by Tijou. Here, on Kent's trompe l'oeil walls, long dead courtiers lean in the arches of colonnades to watch the passing tourists.

The stately *King's gallery*, designed by Wren with a ceiling by Kent has, over its mantelshelf, an intricate dial which has pointed which way the wind blows since 1695. From this grandeur you move straight into the fussy prettiness of the *Duchess of Kent's drawing room*, which she and the young Princess Victoria shared; and then to its ante room with Queen Victoria's Georgian dolls' house and remarkably well-preserved toys. *Victoria's bedroom*, originally the *King's state bedchamber*, is furnished in the style of her time and is full of mementoes of her. It was from this room that she was called to hear the news of her accession. Her babies, and those of Queens Alexandra and Mary, slept in the beautiful curtained cradle.

In the *King's drawing room*, under the ornate Kent ceiling, stands a wondrously elaborate clock which once played music by Handel and now can't even tell the time. The view from the window includes the statue of the young Victoria sculpted by her daughter Louise.

The *council chamber* is a museum of artefacts shown at the Great Exhibition, including a painting of its inauguration, a fairytale ivory throne and footstool from India, and a silver-gilt table centrepiece with some of Queen Victoria's dogs gathered near its base.

Return through the King's drawing room to the magnificent circular *cupola room*, designed in the grand manner by Kent, the ceiling cunningly painted to look even higher than it actually is.

From here you return to the privy chamber and retrace your steps to the Queen's staircase and the exit.

Open 09.00–17.00 Mon–Sat; 13.00–17.00 Sun. Closed some Nat Hols. Charge.

Kenwood House

Hampstead La NW3. 01-348 1286/7. The fine Adam house at the edge of Hampstead Heath, flanked by flower gardens and facing lawns that slope down to the lakeside, was bequeathed to the nation by the first Earl of Iveagh, together with his rich collection of paintings. There is a discreet bookstall in the front hall. Turn left and you find stairs leading up to the *Lady Maufe collection* of 18thC shoe buckles and the *Hull Grundy collection* of heavy 18thC and 19thC jewellery. Downstairs again the beautifully pro-portioned rooms, their long windows looking on to ordered greenery and great trees, open invitingly out of each other. On display are paintings by Reynolds, Romney, Raeburn, Lawrence – Vermeer's *Guitar Player* under the solemn gaze of Rembrandt's *Self-Portrait*, Frans Hals' quizzically smiling *Man with a Cane* – Van Dyck, Pater, Boucher, Turner, Joseph Wright of Derby, and Claude de Jongh's *Old London Bridge*. The orangery, whose dwarf trees produce flowers and fruit, is hung with Gainsboroughs, and from the platform at one end music and poetry recitals are held on *spring and autumn Sun evenings* (details on 01-633 1707). In summer, symphony concerts compete with the birdsong at the lakeside (details on 01-633 1707).

The coach house to the east of the building has the public lavatories and a spacious cafeteria for food and light refreshments which may be enjoyed indoors with the coach or outside among the sparrows and rooks. Talks on the collection can be arranged. (Charge for concerts and reci-tals.)

Open 10.00–19.00 Mon–Sun Apr–Sep; 10.00–17.00 Mon–Sun Feb, Mar & Oct; 10.00–16.00 Mon–Sun Nov–Jan. Free.

Kew Palace

Kew Gardens, Richmond Surrey. 01-940 7333. The Dutch House, as it is sometimes called, was built in 1631 for a merchant called Samuel Fortrey. In 1802 George III and Queen Charlotte used it while they awaited the building of a new Summer Palace, which was never completed. The Queen in particular loved the chunky brick house – and died here in 1818.

Tickets etc in the entrance hall. Then turn right into the *King's dining room*, with the Tudor rose in its ceiling. The *King's breakfast room*, next door, has the original 17thC panelling and a Bogdani picture of flying ducks over the mantel. Climb the stairs and, before going into the *Queen's boudoir*, look up the next flight past the 18thC lantern to admire the portrait of George III – not a painting but a needlework picture. In the boudoir pay your respects to the King and Queen by way of their portraits by Zoffany. In the *Queen's drawing room* empty chairs are grouped politely around a Tschudi harpsichord, as though a ghostly musical evening is about to begin. Continue through the ante room with the King's wig closet and into his *bedchamber* where the dressing table is actually his. In the Queen's more splendid *bedchamber*, the chair where she is said to have died still stands by the window. Beyond it a pretty ante room gives a good view on to the formal gardens below, laid out in the 1960s in 17thC style and worth a visit on their own account.

Go down the stairs and follow signs to the *pages waiting room* with its exhibition of royal knick-knacks, including a heavy silver rattle fit to brain a baby and an illustrated family tree from George I to Victoria. Next is the *library* (though the only books are hiding behind the door) with a case full of George IV's fishing tackle and paintings of Kew Gardens. Exit through a tiny ante-room whose linenfold panelling has been carefully restored.

Don't miss the chance to explore the 300 acres of the Royal Botanic Gardens which spread south from the palace. They are an important research institute and a wonderful sight with more than 25,000 species and varieties of plants and two exceptionally fine Victorian glass houses. Decimus Burton designed the magnificent curved iron and glass palm house and temperate house (1844–48), while the pagoda is by Sir William Chambers (1760). Also two attractive cafeterias.

Gardens open 10.00–20.00 (16.00 winter) Mon–Sun; small charge. Palace open 11.00–17.30 Mon–Sun, Apr–Sep. Closed Oct–Mar, Good Fri & May Day. Charge.

Lancaster House 5 K 18

Stable Yd, St James's SW1. Begun by Smirke in 1820 for the Grand Old Duke of York (who quarrelled with his architect and appointed Benjamin Wyatt in his place), and known at first as York House. When it was acquired by the first Duke of Sutherland, formerly Marquess of Stafford, it was renamed Stafford House. In 1912 the first Viscount Leverhulme bought it for the nation and named it after his home county. Its decorous town-house exterior is no real preparation for the truly luscious Baroque splendours of its interior. This, and the fact that it is now used as a government and state hospitality centre, give it the air of an exceptionally fine hotel of the old school.

The centrepiece is Sir Charles Barry's magnificent staircase which draws the eye up to a lavishly decorated ceiling supported by black caryatids. Moving through the lower rooms to the left you come first to the *Garibaldi room*, with its medallion commemorating his visit, with the *east dining room* to the left, and to the right the *state dining room* whose 18thC French clock is said to have belonged to Napoleon. Continue through the *red* and *gold rooms* and back to the vestibule with its wind dial worked by the weathervane on the roof. On the flamboyantly decorative upper floor, the *west ante room* leads to the *west drawing room*, its ceiling painting of the solar system by H. Howard RA. Back through the *west ante room* is the *state drawing room* with its wonderful coffered ceiling. The *east ante room* leads into the enormous and sumptuous *great gallery*. Its ceiling painting of *St Crisoganus Borne to Heaven by Angels* was borne here from a church in Rome. The *ante room* beyond it has a ceiling painting by Veronese and leads into the richly decorative *music room* where Chopin is said to have entertained Queen Victoria.

Open 14.00–18.00 Sat, Sun & Nat Hols only, between Easter & mid-Dec. Closed at short notice for functions. Free.

Leighton House 1 D 4

12 Holland Pk Rd W14. 01-602 3316. Lord Leighton was a towering figure of Victorian high art. His house, which he designed for himself with the help of Geoffrey Aitchison, has been preserved as a monument both to him and to his contemporaries in art. It is also a most suitable setting for Victorian studies. The barrel-vaulted *studio* on the first floor is frequently used for lectures, poetry readings and musical evenings. The heart of the house is the peaceful *Arab hall*,

left of the entrance. The light is gently broken by Damascus lattice work, the silence by a tiny central fountain. The mosaic frieze is by Walter Crane, but the oriental tiles, upon which the Koran speaks welcoming words in exquisite Arabic script, date from the 14th and 15th centuries and were acquired with the help of the explorer Sir Richard Burton.

In the large entrance hall and on the stairs are displays of William de Morgan tiles and ceramics and paintings by Kensington artists including Burne-Jones and Lord Leighton himself – whose bronze of an athlete can be seen in the secluded garden at the back.

Open 11.00–17.00 Mon–Sat. Closed Sun & Nat Hols. Free.

Linley Sambourne House   **1 D 6**
18 Stafford Ter W8. 01-994 1019. Edward Linley Sambourne was an artist and prominent Punch cartoonist during the late Victorian and Edwardian periods. He lived and worked here for about 40 years, and although the discreet brass plate on the door proclaims him *Not At Home* in a sense he is. His daughter, Mrs Messel, and his granddaughter, Anne, Countess of Rosse, preserved the house, with an affection which is still almost tangibly present, exactly as it was in his time. Here in 1958 the Victorian Society was founded so that when, in 1980, the house was given to the nation, a group of enthusiastic and informed guardians was already on hand. The lively and complex clutter is apparent from the moment the door opens and the fountain is heard at the top of the stairs. The William Morris wallpaper is virtually hidden behind framed Punch cartoons, illustrations for the *Water Babies*, photographs taken for reference, family portraits, Dürer woodcuts and the pictures by contemporaries – Kate Greenaway for one. The beautiful furniture is half hidden and half enhanced by the lamps, clocks, ornaments, vases and fans it supports.

To the right of the door is the dining room – buy tickets and guide books here. Behind it, the morning room, later Lord Rosse's study. Don't fail to go through to the back for a look at the Victorian lavatory (not in use) and the neat garden. Upstairs is the L-shaped drawing room, the heart of the house. Here Sambourne often worked, presumably by artificial light, beside the stained glass windows at one end while family life continued at the other. Go up again to the bedroom used by Lady Rosse – and notice the photograph of Sambourne at work in the room below and the illustrious

signatures on the fireplace fan. Behind is the bedroom used by Sambourne's son Roy and upstairs the bathroom with its coffin-like bath. The top-lit, top-floor studio is not open yet – but may be when the quantities of diaries, photographs and papers have all been checked and catalogued.
Open 10.00–16.00 Wed; 14.00–17.00 Sun, Mar–Oct only. Charge.

Marble Hill House

Richmond Rd, Twickenham Middx. 01-892 5115. An attractive English Palladian house built for Henrietta Howard, mistress of George II and later Countess of Suffolk. It stands near the banks of the Thames in grounds originally designed by Alexander Pope and Charles Bridgeman. The ground and first floors have been redecorated as nearly as possible in their original style and though some of the furniture and pictures are on loan, the GLC is gradually acquiring some permanent furnishings, all dating from the lifetime of the Countess herself. It is hoped that the second floor will eventually be opened to the public, when redecoration is completed.

The front door leads into the staircase hall, with rich mahogany stairs and bannisters to the first floor, and a desk for guide books and cards. Straight ahead is the hall, its ceiling supported by four pillars in true Palladian style. From the hall the breakfast parlour is to the left and the dining parlour to the right, with reproduction wallpaper in the former and an exhibition of plans of the English Palladian movement in the latter. Upstairs the rooms open out of each other so you may circle the first floor, watching the ever-changing views from the windows. The white and gold great room has portraits from the school of Van Dyck and a Thornhill above the mantelpiece. The bed in Lady Suffolk's bedchamber behind its screen of Ionic columns, is dated about 1740 and is on loan from the V & A. Next door is the simple bedchamber of Miss Hotham, a later owner of the house. Across the staircase landing is the damask bedchamber, with reproduction chimneypiece and wallpaper and beyond it the dressing room whose petit-point chairs and settee date from 1760.

From the tea rooms in the nearby coach house (*open Easter–Sep*) you can watch the locals exercising their dogs on the sweeping lawns.
Open 10.00–17.00 Mon–Thu & Sat–Sun. Closed Fri & Christmas. Free.

William Morris House Gallery
Lloyd Park, Forest Rd E17. 01-527 5544 Ext 4390. William Morris, designer, socialist, poet, craftsman and towering figure in the 19thC Arts and Crafts Movement lived here from 1848, when he was 14, until 1856. The reference library and study collection of items not always on show are available to serious students, but please telephone first.

From the hall, hung with framed sections of wallpaper (and with wallpaper postcards and giftwrap for sale) go into the room on the left for displays outlining his life and work. Here are wallpapers, textiles, furniture and much informative text.

The room which opens off it to the right has an exhibition on Morris as book designer, including title pages from publications of the Kelmscott Press. Here, too, are a small collection of William de Morgan tiles and of the heavy pottery of the Martin Brothers, including one of their wryly grotesque birds.

Continue through a small room of tiles and pictures by Ford Maddox Brown and Burne-Jones and you are back in the hall.

The room at the other side of the front door is used for a variety of temporary exhibitions, not always relevant to the house.

Up the magnificent staircase is the *Brangwyn Gift*, with a case of Rodin bronzes on the spacious landing and Brangwyn's own furniture, paintings and china in the two rooms sharp right from the top of the stairs.

Second right off the landing is the *Pre-Raphaelite gallery* with paintings and sketches by Rossetti, Burne-Jones, Ruskin, Lord Leighton, Arthur Hughes, Evelyn de Morgan and Alma-Tadema.

On the opposite side of the landing are the designs in furniture and textiles of A.H. Mackmurdo and the Century Guild, including a showcase of their journal, *The Hobby Horse*. The surrounding park has light refreshments.
Open 10.00–13.00 & 14.00–17.00 Tue–Sat; 10.00–12.00 & 14.00–17.00 on first Sun of each month. Closed Sun, Mon & Nat Hols. Free.

Osterley Park House
Isleworth, Middlesex. 01-560 3918. Built by Sir Thomas Gresham in the 1570s, refurbished by Robert Adam in the 1760s, in the possession of the Earls of Jersey from the start of the 19thC, and presented to the nation by the 9th Earl in

1949. It is now an outpost of the Victoria and Albert Museum and one of the most perfect examples of 18thC decor and furniture in the country.

Hall. In pale grey and white with stucco decoration and statues from Rome.

Gallery. Turn right through this (you return later) and have a look in the tiny green

Turret room, fitted up as a water closet, which opens to the left. Turn right into the

Eating room. This is how guests would have seen it first – the lyre-backed chairs against the walls and the gate-legged tables waiting outside to be brought in with the food, so that nothing should distract from the elaborate design, of which each individual piece of furniture and decoration is an integral part.

Great staircase. The ceiling painting by Rubens has long gone but notice the three magnificent Adam lamps. The stairs go down to the public lavatories and up to the private bedchambers, two of which are shortly to be opened to the public.

Library. Low-relief ceiling with bright decoration, inset paintings on the walls by Antonio Zucchi, fine 18thC furniture possibly by John Linnell.

Breakfast room. Decorated before Adam began on the house, though the pier-glasses and side tables are by him. Retrace your steps to the

Long gallery. Probably by Sir William Chambers who may also have designed the furniture, though the long sofas may be by Adam, who filled in the large windows which were originally at either end.

Drawing room. Richly flamboyant ceiling, its pattern more or less echoed in the Moore carpet. The wall covering is a replica of the original green silk damask. Don't miss the two Reynolds portraits, one each side of the fireplace.

Tapestry room. Drawn curtains and electric candles create the perfect light for the rose-coloured Gobelins tapestries by Jacques Neilson.

State bedchamber. Dominated by Adam's green and gold extravaganza of a bed. But don't neglect to admire the graceful gilded armchairs.

Etruscan dressing room. The only surviving example of this kind of Adam decoration, the walls painted to resemble the patterns on Greek vases, mistakenly known as Etruscan in the 18thC.

Just outside this room is a small exhibition of plans,

photographs, and explanations of the interior and exterior. The grounds, with their lakes and magnificent cedar trees, are freely open until dusk, and the stable block has a cafeteria, open at the same times as the house, from Apr–Sep.

Open 14.00–18.00 Tue–Sun, Apr–Sep; 12.00–16.00 Tue–Sun Oct–Mar. Closed Mon & winter Nat Hols. Charge.

Pavlova Memorial Museum

Ivy House, North End Rd NW11. 01-458 4646. The house where Anna Pavlova lived from 1912 until her death in 1931, and from which she set out on her famous tours, has had several owners since. Some of them have altered it, and not for the better. At present the Middlesex Polytechnic holds sway and the charming and atmospheric exhibition is relegated to a large room on the first floor with a view over the garden and the lake where Pavlova once fed her pet swans. Though there is plenty to see – small pieces of furniture, photographs, playbills, personal possessions – there is more in store. If funds are forthcoming the Pavlova Society (formed by the curator on the basis of the interest aroused by the exhibition) hopes to acquire the whole house and exhibit costumes, make books available, show films, and even perhaps organise dance workshops. Already films and lectures get an airing, from time to time, at Holborn Library, see *Dance and Dancers* for details.

Open 14.00–18.00 Sat. Closed Sun–Thu. Free. Small, so parties should book.

Syon House

London Rd, Brentford Middx. 01-560 0884. A Tudor house, whose main floor was transformed and redecorated by Robert Adam. It was built by the Protector Somerset and, after various changes of ownership, was given to the Percys, Dukes of Northumberland, in perpetuity in 1604. The present Duke still lives here for part of the year. The guides who sit at one end of each of the main rooms can be activated by a single question into being most informative about the house, paintings and furniture.

Great hall. Doric columns, decorative stucco work and antique statues from Rome. The bronze of the *Dying Gaul* is a fine copy, acquired in 1773.

Ante room. In grand Roman style with verde-antique columns, some from the bed of the River Tiber, supporting gilded classical statues, high under an ornate gilded ceiling.

Dining room. White and gold elegance. The marble statues in the niches are copies of antiques chosen by Adam. The gilt brass standard lamps were a gift to the 3rd Duke by the King of Portugal.

Red drawing room. The walls are hung with red Spitalfields silk, the carpet by Thomas Moore of Moorfields is the finest extant example of his work. The portraits, all of Stuarts, include paintings by Huysmans, Lely and Van Dyck.

Long gallery. Long indeed at 136 feet, and lined with valuable books. The portrait medallions below the cornice are of the Northumberlands. The view from the window includes, across the river, part of Kew Gardens, its flagpole dominant.

Oak passage. A picture gallery of royal and family portraits. *Belshazzar's Feast*, painted on glass by John Martin, is at the far end.

West corridor. The window looks onto a central court where Adam would have built a rotunda had funds not failed.

Leading off this is the staircase well. You may not ascend, but may admire the huge Sèvres vase and enormous Rubens canvas opposite it. Don't miss the 18thC sedan chair with the Northumberland lion perched on top. Allow time to explore the 55 acres of parkland with their conservatory, aviary, aquarium, London Butterfly House and excellent Garden Centre.

Grounds open 10.00–18.00 all year round. Charge for Butterfly House. House open 12.00–17.00 (last ticket 16.15) Sun–Thu, Easter–Sep. 12.00–17.00 Sun only, Oct. Closed Fri, Sat & Nov–Easter. Charge.

Wesley's House and Chapel   **6 K 33**

47 City Rd EC1. 01-253 2262. The Chapel was begun in 1777 to replace the first Methodist chapel, opened in an aged converted foundry nearby some 40 years earlier. Described by John Wesley himself as 'neat but not fine' it has changed little, despite renovation and restoration. The original pillars, masts of warships from Deptford docks, the gift of George III, which were plastered and painted to look like marble, have been removed to the vestibule and replaced by genuine marble ones, given by Methodist groups from all over the world. Wesley's own three-decker pulpit is still in place, though lowered now. In front of the chapel stands Adams-Acton's bronze of him, and his grave is to one side. Next door is the house which he and others used in winter – summers being spent in itinerant preaching.

Ring the bell for admittance. The ground floor front has tickets, guide books and information. The ground floor back, a small display of books and letters. The first floor front was Wesley's study, with his bureau, straddle chair, gown and posthumous portrait by Frank O. Salisbury. The first floor back was his bedroom and has a picture of his death with all his visitors grouped as though present simultaneously, and identified in a key below. Off the bedroom stands the tiny, quiet, prayer and meditation room. The second floor back was his brother Charles Wesley's room, complete with bureau, hymn books, letters. The second floor front is the museum room – with the best view of the Nonconformist burial ground opposite, where Defoe, Blake, Bunyan and others lie. Inside is a simple display of personal effects, books, a huge teapot given by Josiah Wedgwood and even the electrical machine Wesley used in the treatment of melancholia. Those who attend Sunday morning service may join in a tour of the house afterwards. *Open 10.00–16.00 Mon–Sat; 12.00 (after service)–15.00 Sun. Charge.*

LIBRARIES

London is well-equipped with libraries. Public libraries, maintained by each borough, have good general collections of reference books and some have large collections on specific subjects. The specialist reference libraries listed below – a selection from a possible 400 or more – are in the main for serious research students. In other words, if you can find what you want in a public library they'd rather you didn't bother them. This is not for reasons of elitism but because of lack of seating space and qualified staff. If you can convince them of your need you will find them charming and helpful. Expect a bag search – on the way in for bombs and on the way out for stolen books.

BRITISH LIBRARY

This is the National Copyright Library which holds one copy of each printed book published in the UK. It is also a wide-ranging reference library with an incomparable collection whose separate departments are listed below. Use of the

Domed Reading Room, British Library

famous domed reading room within the British Museum, known as the Bloomsbury Reading Rooms, is restricted to those with a reader's pass. Apply in person with a letter of recommendation from 'a person of standing'. Due to shortage of space you will only get in if your need is genuine. Your photograph will be taken and you will be barred from certain departments if under 21.

British Library Reference Division   **3 G 24**
Bloomsbury Reading Rooms, British Museum, Gt Russell St WC1. 01-636 1544. More than eight million volumes of European printed books, including everything printed in the UK. *Open 09.00–17.00 Mon, Fri, Sat; 09.00–21.00 Tue–Thu. Closed Nat Hols.* Reader's pass essential.

Department of Manuscripts   **3 G 24**
British Museum WC1. More than 200,000 mss, many of them illuminated, most of them valuable, from the 3rdC BC. (For Egyptian Papyri apply to Department of Egyptian Antiquities.) *Open 10.00–16.45 Mon–Sat. Closed Sun, Nat Hols & last complete week in Oct.* Reader's pass plus special pass from department.

Map Library   **3 G 24**
British Museum WC1. On the mezzanine floor at the north of the building. 10,000 volumes of maps and 500,000 sheet maps of all parts of the world and most dates. *Open 09.30–*

16.30 Mon–Sat. Closed Sun, Nat Hols, last complete week in Oct. Reader's pass and sign the register.

Music Library   3 G 24

British Museum WC1. 01–636 1544. Books about music are usually made available in the Bloomsbury Reading Rooms, though you may be directed to the North Library or the Music Reading Area at the west end of the Official Publications Library. Music manuscripts may be seen in the students room of the Department of Manuscripts.

Newspaper Library

200 Colindale Av NW9. 01-200 5515. UK and overseas newspapers in bound volumes. For London papers prior to 1801 apply to Bloomsbury Reading Rooms. *Open 10.00–17.00 Mon–Sat. Closed Sun, Nat Hols & week following last complete week of Oct.* Apply for pass in person with proof of identity.

Official Publications Library   3 G 24

Bloomsbury Reading Rooms WC1. Near the north entrance to the Museum. Official British publications and political and educational journals. *Open 09.30–16.45 Mon, Fri & Sat; 09.30–20.45 Tue–Thu. Closed Sun, Nat Hols & week starting first Mon in May.* Reader's pass.

Oriental Manuscripts and Printed Books   3 G 24

British Museum WC1. The reading room for the Department is towards the north entrance to the Museum. 40,000 mss and 400,000 printed books in all the literary languages of Asia and North and North East Africa. *Open 10.00–16.45 Mon–Fri; 10.00–12.45 Sat. Closed Sun, Nat Hols & week preceding last complete week in Oct.* Reader's pass.

Science Reference Library   6 J 26

25 Southampton Buildings, Chancery La WC2. 01-405 8721 Ext 3344. Books, pamphlets, periodicals and reports on the inventive sciences, engineering, industrial technologies and commerce. *Open 09.30–21.00 Mon–Fri; 10.00–13.00 Sat.* Ready access, no pass needed.

Foreign Patents Reading Room   6 J 26

Chancery House, Southampton Bldgs WC2. 01-405 8721 Ext 3411. *Open 09.30–17.30 Mon–Fri.* Ready access, no pass needed.

Aldwych Reading Room   6 J 24

9 Kean St WC2. 01-636 1544 Ext 229. Periodicals, books and pamphlets on the life sciences and technologies, medicine, earth sciences, astronomy and pure mathematics. *Open 09.30–17.30 Mon–Fri.* Ready access, no pass needed.

ART AND ARCHITECTURE

British Architectural Library   2 D 21

Royal Institute of British Architects, 66 Portland Pl W1. 01-
580 5533. More than 100,000 volumes on architecture and
related subjects, from 15thC manuscripts to recent publications. Also, more than 400 current periodicals from all over
the world. *Open 10.00–17.00 Mon; 10.00–20.00 Tue–Thu;
10.00–19.00 Fri; 10.00–13.30 Sat.* Their extensive collection
of architectural drawings is 20 minutes walk away in the
Heinz Gallery, 21 Portman Sq W1. 01-580 5533. *By appointment between 10.00–13.00 Mon–Thu.*

British Museum's Department of Prints and Drawings 3 G 24

Gt Russell St WC1. 01-636 1555. To consult the huge
collection of drawings, prints and etchings, acquire a reader's pass by completing a form and supplying a written
reference. Forms by post or from the department itself, on
the 5th floor, above the north entrance. Should they turn
you down, the open gallery has changing exhibitions of
treasures. *Open 14.15–16.00 Mon–Sat.*

Central School of Art and Design Library   3 H 25

Southampton Row WC1. 01-405 1825. Works on the fine
arts, graphic design and industrial design – intended for
students of the school, though anyone may consult the books
in situ. *Open 09.30–19.30. Mon–Thu; 09.30–17.30 Fri;
closed during holidays.*

Courtauld Institute of Art Library   2 D 17

20 Portman Sq W1. 01-935 9292. Book library for students
only, but the two photographic libraries – the Wick Library
of paintings and drawings and the Conway Library of
architecture, applied arts and illuminated manuscripts – are
available to all on request. The Institute's reception desk has
the relevant form. *Open 10.00–17.00 Mon–Sat.*

Fine Arts Library   5 J 21

Central Reference Library, St Martin's St WC2. 01-930
3274. Part of Westminster City Libraries and therefore
public. 25,000 works on painting, sculpture, pottery and
porcelain, furniture, costume, antiques and architecture;
also catalogues from exhibitions and Sotheby's and current
periodicals. The unique Preston Blake collection has more
than 600 volumes on William Blake. *Open 10.00–19.00
Mon–Fri; 10.00–17.00 Sat.*

National Monuments Record 2 H 20
23 Savile Row W1. 01-734 6010. Principally a photographic library, initiated by the Royal Commission on Historic Monuments, covering everything from barns to cathedrals. Also detailed reports on buildings of note or in danger. *Open 10.00–17.30 Mon–Fri.*

Royal Academy of Fine Arts 2 D 21
Burlington House, Piccadilly W1. 01-734 9052. To the right within the main entrance of this last of the great 18thC palaces of Piccadilly (its façade a Victorian–Renaissance addition) is the library of 15,000 volumes on the fine arts. Richest in 18th and 19thC works and anything to do with the Academy itself. Open to members, students and friends of the RA, but ask nicely and they'll let you in. *Open 14.00–17.00 Mon–Fri.*

Royal Society of Arts 6 K 23
6–8 John Adam St WC2. 01-839 2366. The social and economic history of the fine arts in 11,000 volumes and a special collection of catalogues from the great international exhibitions of 1851–1862. Apply by telephone or letter.

Sir John Soane's Museum Library 3 I 25
13 Lincoln's Inn Fields WC2. 01-405 2107. The private collection of the famous neo-classical architect, to which nothing has been added since his death – literature, art, architecture and 15th–19thC architectural drawings, including his own. Write for permission, preferably specifying exactly what it is you want to see.

Victoria and Albert Museum Art Library 1 H 10
Cromwell Rd SW7. 01-589 6371. The national art library of nearly half a million works on art history in all periods and all countries. The Prints and Drawings department covers art, architecture, pure and applied design and graphics. Open to all, though if you plan frequent visits or need to handle rare books you should apply for a ticket (fill in the form at the desk and offer a letter of recommendation from some worthy citizen). *Open 10.00–17.45 Mon–Thu; 10.00–12.30 & 14.00–17.45 Sat; closed Fri.*

DRAMA
British Theatre Centre 2 D 22
9 Fitzroy Sq W1. 01-387 2666. Members only, but you may join on demand for an annual sub. Three libraries (lending, reference and sets department) on three floors offer you

250,000 books on all aspects of theatre, including technique, criticism and printed plays. Also press cuttings for background information and sets of plays for readings. *Open 10.00–17.00 Mon–Fri (19.30 Wed); closed weekends & Aug.*

FILM AND SOUND

British Film Institute   2 I 22
127 Charing Cross Rd WC2. 01-437 4355. The national archive of films, stills, books, scripts and periodicals is open only to members of the Institute, but there is a telephone inquiry service (and someone with a pressing need for information might be admitted).

National Sound Archive   1 H 10
British Institute of Recorded Sound, 29 Exhibition Rd SW7. 01-589 6603. First, make an appointment. Then you will find yourself with access to a free playback service of more than 400,000 discs and 20,000 hours of recorded tape of the RSC, the Aldwych World Theatre Season, drama from the South Bank, the Royal Court, fringe and regional companies and the BBC. *Open 10.30–17.30 Mon–Fri; 21.00 Thu.* The periodical and book library on all aspects of sound is *open 09.30–16.30 Mon–Fri; 21.00 Thu.* No appointment necessary.

GENERAL

London Library   5 J 20
14 St James's Sq SW1. 01-930 7705. Britain's largest subscription lending library from which members may borrow up to 10 of its more than a million volumes, dating from the 16thC. Founded by Thomas Carlyle in 1841 and a boon to writers and scholars. *Open 09.30–17.30 Mon–Sat, to 19.30 Thu.*

HISTORY

Institute of Archaeology   3 E 24
University of London, 31–34 Gordon Sq WC1. 01-387 6052. University department library, with its own entrance. The 20,000 volumes cover most areas of the world. Open to those engaged in bona fide research only. Apply by phone or post.

Institute of Classical Studies   3 E 24
31–34 Gordon Sq WC1. 01-387 7697. Covers all aspects of life in the Graeco-Roman world and incorporates the collections of the Hellenic and Roman societies. The Institute is part of the University and the two societies are

private, so you'll have to prove serious intent before you will be admitted. *Open 09.30–18.00 Mon–Fri; 10.00–17.00 Sat. Times vary in summer.*

Institute of Historical Research 3 F 24
University of London, Senate House, Malet St WC1. 01-636 0272. 100,000 volumes of British and foreign history – indeed, the principal source of same. Members only – apply in writing if you can be sure that access is essential to your research. *Open 09.00–21.00 Mon–Fri; 09.00–17.00 Sat.*

National Maritime Museum Library
Romney Rd, Greenwich SE10. 01-858 4422. Maps, charts, manuscripts and printed books on every aspect of maritime life. Write or telephone first, then present yourself at the Museum's information desk with identification. *Open 10.00–17.00 Tue–Fri; Mon & Sat by appt only.*

LITERATURE

Arts Council Poetry Library 3 J 23
1st Floor, 9 Long Acre WC2. 01-379 6597. English 20thC poetry may be enjoyed in situ or borrowed after you have acquired a ticket. *Open 10.00–17.00 Tue–Sat, 19.00 Fri.*

LONDON

Guildhall Library 6 M 30
Aldermanbury EC2. 01-606 3030. Within the building from which the City is governed is this large public reference library with its extensive collection of works on all aspects of London. *Open 09.30–17.00 Mon–Sat.*

Museum of London Library 6 L 30
London Wall EC2. 01-600 3699. You must telephone for an appointment and you will have to convince them you cannot find what you want at the excellent Guildhall Library, above. They specialise in archaeology, history and topography of London and on subjects covered by their collections – decorative arts, silver, costume etc. Also a section on museology. *Open 10.30–17.30 Mon–Fri.*

MUSIC

Central Music Library 5 M 14
Buckingham Palace Rd SW1. 01-730 8921. A public reference library, part of Westminster City Libraries, with a rich collection of scores and printed books, the majority relating to classical music. *Open 09.30–19.00 Mon–Fri; 09.30–17.00 Sat.*

PHOTOGRAPHIC

Design Council Slide Library   5 J 21
28 Haymarket SW1. 01-839 8000. Some 40,000 slides and prints, for reference or reproduction, on all aspects of design, historical and modern. Ready access. *Open 10.00–17.00 Mon–Fri.*

Radio Times Hulton Picture Library   2 D 19
35 Marylebone High St W1. 01-580 5577. More than six million photographs are stored here, on every possible subject, for professional reproduction. A telephone appointment is essential. *Open 09.30–17.00 Mon–Fri.*

PRINTING

St Bride Printing Library   6 L 27
St Bride Institute, Bride La EC4. 01-353 4660. A public reference library of books on graphic design, papermaking, printing, binding and everything to do with the construction of books. *Open 09.30–17.30 Mon–Fri.* The exhibition room, which is not always in use, is *open 10.00–17.00 Mon–Fri.*

PUBLIC RECORDS

Public Record Office Library   6 K 26
Chancery La WC2. 01-405 0741. The search rooms contain legal documents and government archives from Domesday Book to 1800. Material from 1800 onwards is stored in their building in Ruskin Av, Kew. Present yourself at the enquiries desk, in either case, with proof of identity and ask for a reader's ticket. *Open 09.30–17.00 Mon–Fri.* The ever-popular Census Returns may be viewed on a more readily available day pass at the Land Registry Building in Portugal St, five mins from Chancery Lane. *Open 09.30–16.50.*

MUSEUMS ═══════════

London's national museums are among the richest in the world – and they're free. The material they own is not all on view, there is usually a significant amount stored away for lack of display space – although access to it is available to anyone with a genuine interest. The British Museum and the V & A will give expert opinions on the age or identity of objects, but not valuations. All have reference libraries which are described in the previous chapter.

There are also a great many smaller specialist museums – some built out of the collections of private individuals, some attached to churches or institutions. Some are free, some charge, most welcome a donation towards upkeep or the acquisition of new objects. Expect a baggage search on the way in, and be prepared in some cases to leave large bags and umbrellas in the cloakroom.

There is not the space here to detail every item on show – so the aim has been to give a general idea of the scope of a particular collection and to draw attention to some of the outstanding items. However, museums do rearrange their galleries and sometimes close them at short notice for maintenance or redecoration – so if planning a long pilgrimage to a particular exhibit a preliminary telephone call would be wise.

NATIONAL COLLECTIONS

British Museum   3 G 24
Gt Russell St WC1. 01-636 1555. The imposing building by Sir Robert Smirke, which went up in 1823–47, is one of the largest and greatest museums in the world. Its treasures are so rich and varied that no one should even attempt to see them all in a single visit. Be sure to pick up the free leaflets at the information desk to discover the times of the day's lectures, films and gallery talks and the subjects of special exhibitions. And don't miss a look in at Sidney Smirke's magnificent domed reading room (*tour on the hour from 11.00–16.00*). Galleries are arranged as follows: Egyptian: 25, 60–66. Greek and Roman: 1–15, 22 & 23, 68–73. Western Asiatic: 16–21, 24, 26, 51–59. Prehistoric and Romano British: 35–40. Medieval and Later: 41–47, 71. Oriental: 34, 74, 75. Coins and Medals: 50. Prints and Drawings: 67. British Library Galleries 29–33.

1: Cycladic room, with simple, marble female figurines, their arms clamped firmly across their stomachs.

2: Greek Bronze Age. Minoan and Mycenean antiquities.

3: Archaic Greece, from 1000 to 500 BC. Closed for rebuilding until early 1985. Bronze statuettes, decorated pots, pictorial jars.

4: Room of the Kouroi. Closed for rebuilding until late 1984. One marble *kouros*, or young man, is from Boeotia, the other from Cyprus.

5: Room of the Harpy tomb. The tomb, from the top of a funerary pillar in Xanthos, is decorated with smiling harpies, beaming the souls of the dead up to heaven.

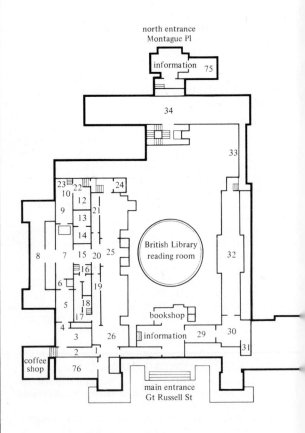

British Museum
plan of ground floor

north entrance
Montague Pl

information   75

34

33

23
22   24
10
12
9   21
13
14
8   7   15   20   25
16
6   19
5   18
17
4
3
26

British Library
reading room

32

bookshop

information   29   30

31

coffee
shop
76

main entrance
Gt Russell St

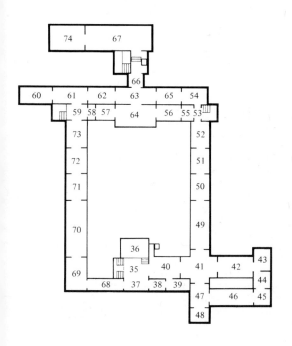

British Museum
plan of upper floors

6: The Bassae room, up some stairs, is encircled by a 400 BC marble frieze from the temple at Bassae showing Greeks in fierce conflict with centaurs and Amazons.

7: Nereid room. Here is the reconstructed façade of a tomb from Xanthos. Its guardian lions' lower jaws seem to have dropped off with 23 centuries of roaring.

8: The Duveen gallery houses the controversial sculptures from the Parthenon (atop the Acropolis in Athens). Lord Elgin bought and brought the marbles to England – there are those in Greece who suggest we give them back.

9: Room of the Caryatid. She and five others once supported the porch of the Erecthion in Athens.

10: Payava room. The entire tomb of Payava the Lycian, transferred here from Xanthos, can also be viewed from another angle when you go up the stairs at 23 to the Etruscan art room.

11: Etruscan art room. Sculpture, pottery, jewellery, paintings and the 2ndC BC sarcophagus of one Seianti, whose effigy seems somewhat startled by death.

12: Mausoleum room. The Tomb of Mausolus was one of the seven wonders of the ancient world. Here are sections of its sculptural frieze, remains of colossal statues and the head of one of four marble horses who drew a chariot at its apex.

13: Hellenistic room. A bronze of Sophocles, a relief of the apotheosis of Homer and a marble Demeter from Cnidus.

14: Roman art. The beautiful cameo glass of the Portland Vase which inspired Wedgwood. Also frescoes, busts and a huge 1stC Apollo (who would be playing his lyre if his arms hadn't dropped off).

15: Roman Art. A marble crouching Aphrodite of the 1stC AD seems to admire a 2ndC mosaic floor.

16: Khorsabad. The colossal winged bulls with the prim, kindly human faces once guarded a city gate at Khorsabad; now landmarks for the stairs down to the lecture theatre.

17: Assyrian Saloon. Sculptures of Ashurnasirpal II, founder of the Assyrian Empire, and vivid bas reliefs of painfully realistic lion hunts.

18: Down to the *Assyrian basement* for more scenes of massacre and mayhem, cases of excavated lion-shaped weights and guardian figures.

19/20: Nimrud. Bas reliefs from the palace of Ashurnasirpal of scenes from daily life – the preparation of the royal meals and the dispatch of the royal enemies.

21: Nineveh. Sculptures from the palace of Sennacherib of the sack of a Chaldean city, in which the waters teem with fish, the land with prisoners and arrows.

22: Stairs down to Greek and Roman architectural mouldings and inscriptions.

23: Stairs up to *Etruscan art* at 11.

24: Ancient Palestine. The Dead Sea Scrolls and a reconstruction of a bronze age tomb from Jericho, six of whose seven skeletons may have been failed grave robbers.

25: The hugely impressive *Egyptian sculpture gallery.* Here are the Rosetta Stone which made the decipherment of hieroglyphics possible; the great granite torso of Rameses II; towering columns from Heracleopolis; false temple doors; the gilded coffin of Lady Henutmehit; rams, lions, a giant scarab, gods and scribes and kings.

26: Assyrian transept. Gateways, gates and guardians of massively impressive proportions. The human-headed winged bulls and winged lions have five legs – so you can see four from the side and two from the front.

29/33 (There is no 27/28). Here are the *British Library galleries* including the splendid *King's gallery* in 32 (constructed for George III, given to the nation by George IV) and the *Map gallery* at 33. Displays change but the dazzling *Lindisfarne Gospels*, the *Gutenberg Bible*, *Magna Carta* and Shakespeare's *First Folio* are always on show. The philately collection is in course of arrangement at the end of 32.

34: Art of China and Japan, South and South East Asia and Islam. Travel clockwise around the first half of the gallery, before the well, and you will pass through these dynasties: Shang 1700–1050 BC; Western Zhou 1050–771BC; Eastern Zhou 770–221; Han 206 BC–220 AD; Han and T'ang Tomb Models; T'ang 619–906; Song 960–1279. At the end, a case of white Ding ware. Turn left through the Jin and Yuan dynasties; left again past delicate lacquer and inlay work and down the other side, past cases of Ming 1368–1644; the art of the Quing dynasty 1644–1912; the Japanese collection, including the *Hull Grundy gift of netsuke*; and into Korea. Beyond the well travel clockwise around the rich collections of SE Asia through India and Pakistan; the Buddhist sculptures and priceless *reliquary of Gandhara*; the Kusham Empire, the Gupta dynasty, Western India, Central India, Kashmir, Eastern India and Orissa, Deccan, South India (the stone Garuda and bronze seated Siva are masterpieces) Sri Lanka, Burma, Thailand, Cambodia, Java. The Islamic Collection at the far end includes mosque lamps and ivories, an astrolabe from Cairo, a jade tortoise from Northern India, pottery and metalwork.

35: Prehistory and Roman Britain, with a centrepiece of a mosaic pavement of the 4thC AD from Hinton St Mary in Dorset; the earliest known Roman representation of Christ.

36: Up the stairs to *Man before metals*. Flint, naturally, and also a grave of 1800 BC.

37/39: Later European prehistory. Bronze vessels, the fine Celtic *Witham shield*, the bits and pieces (literally) for chariotry, and an *Iron Age burial* from Welwyn Garden City.

40: Roman Britain. Much new on display for the first time including the *Thexford Treasure* and items from the Stonea excavations. Also the superb silver of the *Mildenhall Treasure*.

41: Early Medieval. Closed for refurbishing – should open during 1984. Here will be the *Franks casket*, a whalebone box carved with runes; the *Lycurgus cup* and the contents of the *Sutton Hoo ship burial*.

42: Medieval room. Objects with romance in their names – the *Savernake Horn*, the *Royal Gold Cup of the Kings of England and France*, the *Lothar Crystal*.

43: Medieval tile and pottery room, with the 15thC *Canynges pavement* from Bristol at its centre.

44: Gallery of clocks and watches. Timepieces from the Middle Ages to the 19thC.

45: Waddeson Bequest, left by Baron Ferdinand de Rothschild in 1898. Much florid gold and ostentation.

46: Renaissance corridor. Jewellery, silver, enamel and scientific instruments from the Renaissance to the 18thC. Don't miss Mary Queen of Scots' signet ring.

47: Renaissance and later. Pottery, glass and the *Hull Grundy gift of jewellery* – cameos, enamels, chatelaines, hair lockets, watches and Art Nouveau ornaments.

48: Modern gallery. Late 19thC to mid 20thC decorative arts. Glass, ceramics and metalwork.

49: Special exhibitions gallery.

50: Coins and medals. The numismatist's dream, 2000 years worth of shekels, sovereigns, pennies, groats and all.

51/52: Ancient Anatolia and Iran. Gold jewellery from Carchemish, the *Oxus treasure of Persian goldwork*, and some small and appealing bronzes.

53: The Neo-Hittite landing (a situation rather than an event) of sculptural remnants.

54: Ancient Babylonia – The *royal tombs of Ur*. The jewellery, weapons and mosaics of the Sumerians and

Babylonians, all considerably more than 4,000 years old. Also the strangely sinister Sumerian *Goat and Tree*.

55: Western Asiatic prehistory. Tools, pots and the *Jericho skull*.

56: Room of writing. Tablets inscribed with cuneiform and alphabetic scripts, and a sizeable chip off the *Epic of Gilgamesh*.

57: Syrian room, guarded by the statue of *Idrimi the King*. Behind him – sculpture, bronze, jewellery.

58: Nimrud ivories. Intricate carvings from the one-time capital of the Assyrian Empire.

59: Ancient South Arabia. At the top of the stairs stand the limestone heads and inscribed tablets.

60/61: Egyptian mummies. Here they lie, the ancient dead, their tightly bandaged forms often removed from the painted sarcophagi and presented to the common gaze. In 60 there are similarly enwrapped cats, goats, falcons, dogs and ducks. In 61 a desiccated pre-dynastic burial.

62: Egyptian tomb paintings and funerary equipment, now divorced from the corpses they failed to protect. Also papyri, including sheets of the *Book of the Dead of Ami* from which the frieze in the previous two rooms was copied.

63: From death into daily life. Furniture, cosmetics, gaming pieces and delightful models of people at work.

64: Pre dynastic and early dynastic. Seals, scarabs and pretty jewellery.

65: Small sculptures and statuettes of animals, of deities, and of animal deities – especially cats.

66: Coptic corridor. Portraits in plaster and paint, textiles and jewellery.

67: Department of Prints and Drawings. The permanent collection is not on public show but from time to time you will be admitted to view small, special exhibitions.

68: Greek and Roman bronzes and terracottas, some grotesque, many lifelike.

69: Greek and Roman life room, with a noisy little fountain, jewellery displayed on the balcony, writing tablets, toys, military equipment and a 2ndC marble of Mithras slaying the bull in an exceedingly relaxed manner.

70: The image of Augustus. Start at the end nearest to 71 and work back to get an idea of the development of Roman portraiture.

71: The Sutton Hoo ship burial makes an unexpected appearance here – while it awaits removal to room 41 sometime after the end of 1984.

British Museum, South Front

72/3: Greek vases, decorated with lively and often humorous classical scenes.
74: Special exhibitions.
75: Loder gallery, given over to a bequest of Islamic art; luxuriously gleaming Persian, Turkish and Moorish lustreware.
76: New wing gallery for special exhibitions.
The licensed cafeteria, which opens half an hour later and closes half an hour earlier than the museum, serves hot meals at lunchtime, snacks and drinks at all times.
Open 10.00–17.00 Mon–Sat; 14.30–18.00 Sun. Films Tue–Fri; lectures Tue–Sat; Gallery talks daily. Free.

Geological Museum   **1 H 10**
Exhibition Rd SW7. 01-589 3444. This is the national museum of Earth Science, a part of the Institute of Geological Sciences, its collections drawn from all over the world, though with one whole floor devoted to British geology.
The bookshop, inquiry counter, cloakroom and rest lounge are in the entrance hall, with the public lavatories straight ahead and sharp right. No refreshments – try the Science or Natural History museums or the V & A. The library, at the far end of the ground floor, is open for public reference

between *10.00 and 16.00 on weekdays*. There are lectures and films at *14.30 on Tue–Thu & Sat*, on the first floor, and demonstrations and talks for groups, especially school groups, can be arranged with the Education Officer.

Ground floor. Here are the most dramatic and beautiful displays – things get more specialised as you ascend. Straight ahead is the world-famous *Gem and Ornamental Stone collection*, arranged in glowing showcases like a stage set for Aladdin. Beyond, behind a simulated Scottish rock face, is the most fundamental of all exhibitions – *Story of the Earth*. Don't miss having a farewell go on the earthquake simulator to shake yourself back to the present. To find the hidden stairs to the mezzanine floor, with its British fossils and toy dinosaurs, go up the stairs from the entrance and left towards the stalactites.

First floor. The regional geology of Britain set out in a series of individual bays. To find London and the Thames valley go up the main staircase and look to your right.

Second floor. The world's largest display of metalliferous ores and non-metallic minerals and also a collection of building stone. A chance to have a close look at iron, gold, silver and salt in their crude forms.

Open 10.00–18.00 Mon–Sat; 14.30–18.00 Sun. Free.

Imperial War Museum 6 Q 23

Lambeth Rd SE1. 01-735 8922. An extremely popular national museum on all aspects of warfare, military and domestic, concerning Britain and the Commonwealth from 1914. The essentially unquiet nature of its displays is given a further dimension by the fact that it is housed in the central portion of the old Bethlehem Royal Hospital for the Insane – the Bedlam that inspired the final horrific scenes of Hogarth's *Rake's Progress*. The two outer wings were demolished in the 30s, which is why the present building looks somewhat unbalanced.

The displays are currently undergoing a major and long-term reorganisation, but you may be sure of seeing the following: *the First World War*, with a reconstruction of a scene on the Western Front, one of the buses commissioned as troop carriers, guns, equipment, T.E. Lawrence's photographs of the campaign in the Middle East, a Bristol F2B fighter and emotional recruiting posters. *Between the wars*, including an audio visual show on the rise of Fascism. *The Second World War* with a Spitfire, a Fokker, a fishing boat that took part in the evacuation from Dunkirk, tanks, resistance equipment, a German one-man sub, Montgomery's caravan and vivid recreations of life in war-time Britain – gas masks, ration books, Anderson shelters and all. There are also small exhibitions on the Korean, Arab-Israeli, Vietnam, Falkland and other more recent conflicts, and a tableau of a domestic fall-out shelter which is all the more chilling because it looks so cosy.

On the upper floors is the *art gallery* with a selection of intensely dramatic war paintings, including works by Paul Nash, Wyndham Lewis, Dame Laura Knight and Stanley Spencer.

The basement shop has model kits and books as well as the usual guides and cards. There are public film shows at weekends. The reference section includes departments of Documents, Film, Photographs, Printed Books (a national reference library) and Sound Records (a national archive), all available for study by appointment.

The museum has two out-stations – HMS Belfast in the Pool of London, *open 11.00–17.30 (16.30 in winter); closed Nat Hols. Charge.* And Duxford Airfield in Cambridge, *open Mar–Oct 11.00–17.30, or dusk if earlier. Charge. Imperial War Museum open 10.00–18.00 Tue–Sat (17.00 in winter); 14.00–17.30 Sun (17.00 in winter). Closed Mon & Nat Hols. Free.*

Museum of London   **6 L 30**
London Wall EC2. 01-600 3699. The story of the capital from prehistory to the present day, laid out in an ultra-modern setting. Although you walk through history chrono-logically, you may wander at will within each 'age' so that you enjoy something of the sense of discovery. From the entrance, the book counter is ahead, past the bag check, the cloakroom to the right, and the small coffee and snack bar is discovered downstairs at the left, with the lecture theatre and WCs en route (the latter are also in Prehistory!).

Go straight ahead for *The Thames in Prehistory* with its pottery urns, bronze swords, iron daggers and reconstruc-tion of Heathrow as it was in 600 BC.

Beyond is *Roman Londinium* decorated with the leavings of its military founders – and a Roman kitchen and brace of dining rooms mocked up around the delicate mosaic of the Bucklersbury pavement.

Saxon and Medieval London offers brooches, axes, 1066, a model of the Tower, the *Cheapside hoard*, like a dream of a dressing up box, trade, guilds and the horrors of pestilence and civil war. And all to a background of Medieval musak.

Tudor and early Stuart London was prosperous so here are silver plate, Delftware, pewter and other riches. Here too the stews of Bankside, Oliver Cromwell's calm death mask, a complete panelled room from Wandsworth, the Plague, and an effective diorama of the Great Fire with a recorded reading of Samuel Pepys' graphic description as background. About the middle of the Stuart period you will encounter a glass walled ramp leading downwards. (It passes the Lord Mayor's state coach but this is intended as a grand finale and you're not supposed to look at it yet). At the foot of the ramp turn left down some steps, right down three more and straight ahead into late Stuart London – from which you keep working to the left, as upstairs, to keep the story in sequence.

Late Stuart London. A time of reconstruction after the fire, the building of the lovely Wren churches and St Paul's, of the Restoration and a swelling population, of advances in navigation and astronomy, all illustrated with a wealth of material.

Georgian London. The time of Boswell and Johnson, Goldsmith, Hogarth, Reynolds, Smollett, pleasure gardens, evangelism, public executions, the Gordon Riots and the founding of Kew Gardens.

Early 19thC London. Violent contrasts of wealth and poverty, the coronation of Queen Victoria, the Great Exhibition in the Crystal Palace in Hyde Park (later moved to Sydenham), the formation of the metropolitan fire brigade, the police force and the Salvation Army.

Imperial London. Marvel at the growth of the docks, the railways, international communications, the business world. Window shop in the street mock-up, which includes a grocer's, a draper's, a tobacconist, a bank and pub, and see what was offered on a night out at the music hall.

20thC London. Newspapers discovered human interest, women got the vote, the world went to war twice, London transport and Penguin books became commonplace sights and the Festival of Britain opened with a massive firework display on the South Bank.

Ceremonial London. Now you're allowed to look at the splendid state coach of the Lord Mayor. Here are mementoes of lavish royal and state occasions – the present Queen's coronation glove, Queen Victoria's crown (minus jewels) and souvenirs from coronation mugs downwards.

There are regular lectures and events – live madrigals among the Stuart exhibits for example – and the library is available to serious students, as is the Department of Prints and Drawings and the findings of the two archaeological units. *Open 10.00–18.00 Tue–Sat; 14.00–18.00 Sun. Closed Mon. Free.*

Museum of Mankind   **2 I 19**
6 Burlington Gdns W1. 01-437 2224. This building by Pennethorne, originally intended as the HQ of the University of London and decorated with statues of the learned – Newton, Galileo and Archimedes among them – now houses the British Museum's Department of Ethnography. Its huge collections of carvings, artifacts, clothing, weapons and masks from Africa, Australia, the Pacific Islands, the Americas and parts of Asia and Europe are displayed in major exhibitions, each of which is changed after a year or 18 months. Typical was a reconstruction of a village in Gujerat in Northern India with real, live craftspersons weaving and carving outside the realistic huts. Any items not currently on display can usually be made available to scholars and the reference library, open to all, is the largest on the subject in Britain. On the lighter side – children love it for its 'toy-town' reproductions of other cultures and for the magical-mystery flavour of its fetishes, its decorated skulls from Mexico and its American Indian war bonnets and peace pipes.

There are free film shows on Tue–Fri afternoons, linked to the current exhibitions, and anyone may ask for a special showing of anything on the available list – *Eskimo Life*, perhaps, or the *Lost World of the Maya*, or *Nigerian Divination*.

Turn left for the bookshop, film theatre, students' room. Right for the cloakroom, information desk and ground floor exhibitions. Ladies and Gents are each side of the staircase up to the main exhibition halls on the first floor.

No cafeteria, but access to a room in which you may eat your own picnic. *Open 10.00–17.00 Mon–Sat; 14.30–18.00 Sun. Closed Nat Hols. Free.*

National Maritime Museum
Romney Rd SE10. 01-858 4422. This is the world's largest museum on its subject, whose purpose in life is the study and display of material on all imaginable aspects of Britain's maritime history. It must also rank as one of the most beautiful museums anywhere, its main buildings set in a sloping riverside park, with the group which make up the

Old Royal Observatory at the top of the hill behind. It has paintings, scale models, actual vessels, uniforms, swords, medals, navigational and astronomical instruments. It's a sea monster of a place, but don't allow it to daunt – its life-size displays and packed showcases are among the most exciting anywhere.

As you face it, with the Observatory behind, the central building is the Queen's House, a Palladian masterpiece by Inigo Jones. To its left is the east wing and to its right the larger west wing, each joined to it by an elegant covered colonnade.

The colonnade leads to the east wing entrance. A small bookshop is just inside, and immediately after it a series of galleries dealing with the migration to North America and Canada under sail; the history of British sailing vessels; the advent of steam and of the cargo liner; and life at sea from 1840–1960. On the floor below is the chilly story of Arctic exploration, especially the search for the North West Passage and the North Pole. On the upper floor are two rooms of 19thC marine paintings followed by the story of the development of the Royal Navy.

Here, too, is the lecture theatre and the education centre for school parties and the occasional adult evening class. The Queen's House will be closed for redecoration for much of 1984, and its exhibits will be rearranged, but they will still include the *Barberini collection* of 17thC scientific instruments, beautifully executed models of sailing ships, the *Solebay tapestry* from Mortlake, two of whose companions are at Hampton Court, and many of the museum's most important paintings. The centrepiece of the house itself is the great hall. The carved beams are original but the ceiling painting of the school of Thornhill replaces earlier panels now at Marlborough House.

The west wing, entered at the other end of the colonnade, has the main bookshop, the information desk and the entrance to the Caird library and reading room. The best way to proceed is to go straight down to the New Neptune Hall whose prized possession is the complete paddle tug, *Reliant*, surrounded by the story of wooden boat building from prehistory, with several complete ships. Nip down under the bows of *Reliant* for a look at dioramas of the iron and steel shipyards. From the New Neptune Hall go through the Barge House, featuring the glamorous golden form of the 18thC barge of Prince Frederick. You will then find yourself in a series of ground floor galleries. The first takes the history of ship building through its important 15thC stage. The second sports findings from the museum's Archaeological Research Centre. The next three go off on a different tack to present the *National Museum of Yachting*, and the last has a model of the gunship *Cornwallis* and a series of audio visual shows on her construction and navigation.

At the top of the main staircase are three large galleries telling the story of naval and merchant shipping during the first half of the 18thC, with a grand finale of the Royal Dockyards. Go down the stairs at the end and work your way through the tale of James Cook, with Nathaniel Dance's famous portrait; the maritime history of the settlement of the US and the American Revolution; the French Revolution; and at last two Nelson galleries, with the rigging of the *Cornwallis* rearing up from the floor below in the second one.

Don't miss the History of Navigation at the south end of the west wing, near the restaurant.

You are now ready for an assault on the Old Royal Observatory, achieved after a literally breathtaking climb up its green hill. The group of buildings is made up of the Great Equatorial building, with the seventh largest refracting telescope in the world; the Altazimuth pavilion; the South building with its planetarium; and the two which are open to the visitor, Flamsteed House and the Meridian building.

The former, built by Wren and topped by the octagon room observatory, has been furnished more or less as it may have been when the first Astronomer Royal lived in it. A series of modern galleries built on at the back show the history of time-keeping, navigation and surveying by means of displays of elegant instruments, with a ticking, whirring section on clocks and watches below. In the Meridian building, through which runs the line from which all time is measured, is a unique display of instruments (many with dummies peering intently into them) illustrating the history of the measurement of time and the beginnings of the understanding of space.

In the Dolphin Coffee Shop, behind the navigation room, you may eat snacks and light meals between *11.00 and 16.00 Tue–Sat, and between 14.30 and 16.30 on Sun. Open Oct– Easter 10.00–17.00 Tue–Fri; 10.00–18.00 Sat; 14.00–17.30 Sun. Easter–Oct 10.00–18.00 Tue–Sat; 14.00–17.30 Sun. Closed Mon, except Nat Hols. Times may change from Easter 1984. Free.*

National Army Museum   **4 N 10**
Royal Hospital Rd SW3. 01-730 0717. The story of the
British Army from 1480 to 1914, of the Indian Army up to
partition in 1947 and of other Commonwealth armies until
the time of their independence, can be followed in the four
separate galleries. The extension, now in course of building,
will continue the tale from 1914 to the present. From the
entrance, go to the upper foyer for the shop, with its books,
prints, paperweights and model soldiers, and the lavatories.
Go down to the left for the lecture theatre, in use on
Saturdays only, and right to the *weapons gallery* where
examples of most hand-held weapons, from a longbow found
on the Mary Rose to the guns in use today, are displayed in
showcases, dioramas and tableaux. The first floor has the
story proper, from the formation of the Yeoman of the
Guard in 1485 to the beginning of the First World War,
again with much use of models and dioramas of battle
scenes. The skeleton of Napoleon's mount, Marengo, is a
must for those keen to bone up on the anatomy of the horse.
On this floor also is the reading room with an impressive
collection of books, manuscripts, drawings and photographs
– for a ticket, apply in writing to the Director.
The second floor has the *uniform gallery*, in which uniforms
are grouped by periods from 1700–1914. At one end a series
of show cases glitter severely with medals, orders and
decorations. Leading off the uniform gallery is the small *art
gallery* with portraits by Reynolds and Romney among other
British painters.
Open 10.00–17.30 Mon–Sat; 14.00–17.30 Sun. Free.

National Postal Museum   **6 L 29**
King Edward St EC1. 01-432 3851. Behind the statue of Sir
Rowland Hill, originator of the penny post, stands a large
Post Office within which you will encounter one of the
largest and most significant stamp collections in the world.
The main collection, on the top floor, is displayed in rank
upon rank of large frames which slide out from the wall to
reveal the fruits of three major collections. The *Phillips
collection* of 19thC British stamps was the bequest which
made the founding of the museum possible – on account of
its size and quality and the large sum of money that came
with it. It includes sheet upon sheet of Penny Blacks, with
variations so infinitesimal that only the most affectionate eye
can discern them. The *Post Office collection* includes all
stamps issued under its aegis since 1840, plus proof sheets,

designs, trials, recent issues and the stamp archives of the Royal Mint. The *Berne collection* has almost every stamp or piece of postal stationery issued anywhere in the world since 1878.

And don't miss the minor exhibitions on the way up – or down. These include postal memorabilia of the Great Exhibition, the Festival of Britain and other national celebrations; stamp boxes; scales; an ancient blunderbuss used by the postal guards to protect their valuables; and dinky mail vans.

Research facilities are available among the philatelic archives and in the reference library. For the less serious visitor there is a chance to send a postcard which will carry the museum's own postmark. And the Post Office itself has a special window for first day covers to help you keep abreast of developments.

Open 10.00–16.30 Mon–Thu; 10.00–16.00 Fri. Closed weekends & Nat Hols. Free.

Natural History Museum 1 H 9

Cromwell Rd SW7. 01-589 6323. A cathedral-like twin-towered building by Alfred Waterhouse, 1873–80, in pale terra-cotta and slate blue, with animal figures on the outside and a superb Romanesque interior with wild flower decorations all over walls and high curved ceiling. It houses the national collections of zoology, entomology, palaeontology, mineralogy and botany.

Immediately left of the entrance are reception and three excellent shops, for books, souvenirs and guides. To the right the cloakroom and adults-only-rest-area (the need for which becomes obvious as tides of excited young dinosaur-enthusiasts surge to and fro).

Ground floor ahead: The central hall is dominated by *Dinosaurs and their living relatives*, with the apses to the left describing their evolution and extinction by means of push button computer games. To the right of the stairs is the ladies and information desk, to the left the gents, disabled lavatory and children's centre. Behind the stairs is the snack bar and beyond it a corridor lined with stuffed *Fish* and *Reptiles* with the lecture hall off to the left and an entrance to the Science Museum straight ahead. A left turn just before the gents brings you into the *Spider and Scorpion gallery*.

Ground floor left: Past the shops lies the *Bird gallery* with its stuffed cassowaries, eggs, and even a dodo. At the far end, *British Birds* are displayed in small mockups of their habitats

– cliffs, moorland, etc. Returning through birds you pass three turnings to the left. The first leads to *Insects* – learn about the making of honey and silk, butterflies and moths, and some unexpected pests – a cigarette beetle, for example. The second turn leads through *Marine invertebrates* to the *Whale hall*, its models and skeletons predictably large but still overwhelming. The second and third turnings take you to *Human biology* with push-button working models on the body's functions, and a walk-in womb complete with foetus and mother's throbbing heartbeat.

Ground floor right: Past the rest area, a display on the *classification of fossils* leads through *Fossil mammals* to a solemn semi-circle of vast grey hippos, rhinos and elephants. Left from *Fossil mammals*, the series of galleries concerned with ecology, fossil fish, reptiles and invertebrates are due for redevelopment and may already be closed for this.

First floor: Here is the cafeteria. Follow the *Mammal gallery* to the right and take a right turn into the immense and informative display *Origin of species*, with *African mammals* at the far end. On the other hand, the gallery to the left takes you through *Man's place in evolution* with a left turn at the end into a long gallery of glittering *Minerals*, *Rocks* and *Gemstones*, culminating in a dramatic display of glowering meteorites.

Second floor: An exhibition on British natural history, with over 2,000 species of plants, animals and fungi – real specimens and photographs – from the seven main British habitats.

There are regular films and lectures, special exhibitions and events, guide books, information charts and question sheets for children, and a teacher's centre on the first floor where staff will help plan a school visit.

Open 10.00–18.00 Mon–Sat; 14.30–18.00 Sun. Closed Nat Hols in winter & spring. Free.

Science Museum   **1 H 10**

Exhibition Rd SW7. 01-589 3456. Anyone still under the misapprehension that museums are static and boring should visit this vast national collection on science and its applications to industry. Most of the items on display are 'real', not models, large numbers of them still function and are demonstrated daily and, especially in the children's, and the telecommunications galleries, there are buttons to press and levers to pull to put working models through their paces. There are also lectures, film shows and special school holiday events – details from the information office on the ground floor.

You will find cloakroom and museum shop just inside the main entrance, the information office straight through and on the left, public lavatories on ground, first and second floors, and lecture theatres on lower ground and ground floors. The Science Museum Library, specialising in the history of science and technology, is in a separate building round the back at the end of Imperial College Road. To discover the exact whereabouts of items of particular interest invest in the cheap plan from the shop. In general, the lay-out is as follows.

Lower ground floor: children's gallery with working models demonstrating basic scientific principles – and a periscope to spy on the floor above. Also locks, early domestic appliances, all kinds of devices for making fire and a traffic light that responds to your presence.

Ground floor: Weighty displays on power, transport and exploration. There are waterwheels and stationary engines, full-size locomotives, a working signal box, motor cars, a mail coach, eight fire engines, full scale models of a submersible and a moon lander, and the actual *Apollo 10* capsule.

First floor: Hand and machine tools, the history of iron, steel and glass-making, general metallurgy, methods of agriculture, all you've ever wanted to know about gas, and comprehensive displays on meteorology, time measurement, map-making, astronomy (lectures in the star dome when it re-opens) and telecommunications.

Second floor: Here are printing and paper making, lighting, weighing and measuring, chemistry, atomic physics and nuclear power, computing, and science as applied to the sea – navigation, sailing, steam, motor and war-ships, marine engineering, docks and diving.

Third floor: Photography and cinematography from 1835, a good look at optics, heat and temperature, magnetism and electricity, geophysics and oceanography (including a working seismograph), early science and physics and a spacious aeronautics gallery with 22 real aircraft and a catwalk up among the ceiling-suspended, early, lighter-than-air machines.

Fourth and fifth floors: The *Wellcome Museum of the History of Medicine*, with models and full-size reconstructions of surgeons at work from prehistory to today on the lower gallery, and an extraordinary range of related objects in the

upper gallery which illustrate, among other things, how close medicine has always been to witchcraft and torture!
Open 10.00–18.00 Mon–Sat; 14.30–18.00 Sun. Closed Nat Hols in winter & spring. Free.

Victoria and Albert Museum   1 H 10
Cromwell Rd SW7. 01-589 6371. Extravagant Victorian architecture containing more than 10 acres of museum space given over to sumptuous displays of the decorative arts from all categories, countries and centuries. All is not in show-cases. There are also entire rooms – walls, ceiling and all – reconstructed in the galleries and furnished in period style. As the plan provided by the museum shows, the numbering of the galleries is truly eccentric but museum staff are ready with directions and its Friends, at their desk inside the main entrance, have friendly advice and leaflets. Detailed guides to specific collections are in the shop at 49. Rest your dazzled mind and weary feet in the formal central garden. The cafeteria with its wholesome snacks is behind Carpets at 33. There are free lectures daily, usually at *13.15*, in the lecture theatre behind room 67. (Details from Friends.)
The galleries are of two distinct types – primary, which are of most general interest and in which a variety of different types of work are grouped by date or style – and study collections which take the matter further for those with an interest in a particular art or medium.

Primary galleries
1–3: Continental 17thC. Furniture and decorative objects arranged in small, mock rooms.
4–6: Continental 18thC. Including the reconstructed boudoir of Madame de Serilly, containing Marie Antoinette's music stand and work table.
7: Jones collection of 18thC pictures, ceramics and furniture.
8–9: Continental 19thC. More mock-ups of period rooms of Europe.
11–16: Renaissance Italy. Donatello's *Ascension*, Antico's *Meleager*, Luca Della Robbia's 15thC *Stemma of King Rene of Anjou*, a massive wall plaque of high relief heraldry.
Behind 12, 13, 14: The Morris, Gamble and Poynter rooms, designed as the museum's first public refreshment rooms. Morris is green and floral with Burne-Jones stained glass and painted panels. Gamble is tiled in the fanciest of ornamental ceramic work, hugely pillared and mirrored. Poynter is a vision of a Dutch kitchen with blue picture tiles and the original grill.

17–20: Renaissance Italy. Maijolica panels, marquetry chests, a 16thC fresco ceiling, lively terracottas and small marbles.

21–22: High Renaissance, 1500–1600. Breathtaking bronzes and marbles – the head of Pissarro's *Prophet Haggai* whose body is still on the façade of Siena Cathedral; Bernini's *Neptune and a Triton*; Bologna's *Samson slaughtering a Philistine.*

23–24: Gothic art. The magnificence of the early 14thC *Syon Cope*, finely embroidered in silk with gold and silver thread.

25: Spanish art. Hispano–Moresque ware and an early 15thC altarpiece in which St George is suffering such a surfeit of torture it's no wonder he took it out on the dragon.

26–29: Renaissance northern Europe. More sacred than secular. Tomb effigies, tapestries, stained glass and a case of table fountains with most indiscreet water pipes.

32–33: Carpets. Framed, wall-hung and featuring the 16thC Sheldon tapestry maps of Warwickshire.

38: Medieval tapestries. The rich colour and drama of the 15thC Devonshire hunting tapestries.

38a: Japanese art. Ferocious armour, silken robes, intricate netsuke.

40: Costume from the first Elizabethan age to the present one, the groups of elegantly arrayed faceless models divided by cases of lacey fans, parasols and other accessories.

40a: Musical instruments. Beautifully decorated, mostly in working order and recorded. Also clocks, quadrants and music boxes.

41: Indian art, with sculpture in 47A and B adjoining. Hangings, carpets, prints, the superb jade wine cup of Shah Jehan and the mechanical tiger mauling a British officer made to amuse the Sultan of Mysore. In 47B, Siva dances.

42: Islamic art, continuing in 47C adjoining. An inlaid wooden pulpit from Egypt, a gilt glass from Syria known as the *Luck of Edenhall* and the beautiful 16thC Persian mosque carpet from Ardabil.

43: Early Medieval. Jewel studded gospels, ivory crosses and the 12thC *Eltenberg Reliquary*, pillaged from a Benedictine convent during the French Revolution.

44: China and Japan, continuing in 47D adjoining. Calming Buddhas, the red lacquer throne of the Emperor Ch'ien Lung, a T'ang earthenware horse that is all but alive, and Sung and Ming dynasty porcelain.

46: Victorian and Italian cast court, divided by a corridor of fakes and forgeries. The casts include one of Trajan's column in Rome which towers in two halves, the portal of Santiago de Compostele and dreaming effigies – so fragile they all appear to be called 'Do Not Touch'.

48: Raphael Cartoons. These working designs for tapestries, lent by the Queen, are the most significant of the many Renaissance works of art in the museum.

52–54: English Renaissance. A complete English wassail set; the *Great Bed of Ware*; Elizabethan embroidery; Queen Elizabeth's virginals; the Sizergh Castle room, panelled walls, plaster ceiling and all; Torrigiano's terracotta of Henry VII.

55–56: British art 1650–1700. Furniture including an impressive state bed; silver including a toilet service said to have been given to Charles II.

57–58: British art 1700–1750. 18thC English furniture and silver and the elaborately decorated music room from Norfolk House.

118–120: Victorian art. The Harbourne room, with its inlaid panelling; elaborate furniture; sentimental pictures; William Morris; and artefacts shown in the Great Exhibition.

121: Regency. Early 19thC furniture and furnishings.

122–125: British art 1750–1820. The Lee Priory room, an ante room to the Lee Priory library; Robert Adam's lavish glass drawing room from Northumberland House; the dignified Croome Court Library bookcases from Worcestershire.

Study collections.

48: Woodwork study collection.

50: British and Continental sculpture divided by a massive Netherlandish rood loft and containing masterpieces by Nollakens, Roubiliac and Rysbrack.

51: Neo-classical sculpture and a corridor of Rodin bronzes.

62: English alabasters and ivory carvings.

63: Continental sculpture on a small scale.

64: Bronzes.

65–69: English and Continental silver.

70–74: Theatre Museum, in store apart from small temporary exhibitions here, awaiting removal to its new home in Covent Garden Flower Market.

81–82: Pewter and cutlery, base and Sheffield plate from the 14thC to Victoria.

83: Continental church plate.

84: British church plate.

85: Carpets.

87–88: Islamic metalwork and armour.

88a–90: European arms and armour.

91–93: Jewellery. Enter by 93, exit via manned turnstile at *91*. A treasure house of precious exhibits with high security.

94–97: Tapestries, textiles, lace and carpets.

98–99: Oriental textiles and embroidery.

100–101: European textiles and embroidery.

103–106: 20thC study collection.

107: Fans.

109: Embroidery with the tools therefor.

111: Stained glass.

112: Glass vessels.

114: Long gallery of intricate ironwork, English, French, Italian, German and Spanish, and a view down into the Chinese, Islamic and Indian galleries.

116–117: Twin corridors of back-lit *German stained glass.*

128: French ceramics

129: Chinese carvings and glass.

131: Glass vessels.

132: Ancient and South American pottery.

133: Near Eastern pottery.

134–136: Continental earthenware.

137: English earthenware studio pottery.

138: Temporary ceramics exhibitions.

139–40: The finest collection anywhere of *18thC English porcelain and enamels.*

141: European tiles.

142: Continental porcelain.

143–145: Far Eastern pottery and porcelain. Important temporary exhibitions are housed in room 45.

The Henry Cole wing, named for the museum's creator and first director, opened in 1983 for the proper display of the extensive collection of pictures of all kinds. On level 1 is the bookshop. On 2, prints, drawings and temporary exhibitions. On 3, watercolours and a display on the history of photography. On 4, European paintings of the 16th–19th centuries, Gainsborough transparencies, the walk-in panorama of Rome, and the collection of portrait miniatures (the lights, on time switches, are operated by a button on the rail before each case). On 5, the print room for students and those with appointments only. On 6, the crowning glory, the unique collection of Constable drawings and paintings presented to the museum by his daughter.

The Boilerhouse Project (01-581 5273) in the old boilerhouse yard, which is independent of the museum, mounts changing exhibitions on aspects of design.

For the extensive library, see 'Libraries' chapter, and see also separate entries for the branch museums: Apsley House, Bethnal Green Museum of Childhood, Ham House and Osterley Park House.

Open 10.00–17.50 Mon–Thu & Sat; 14.30–17.50 Sun. Closed Fri & some Nat Hols. Free.

Westminster Abbey Treasures 5 N 20

The Cloisters, Westminster Abbey SW1. 01-222 5152. Underneath the abbey is a small museum of plans, seals, charters, prints and documents, together with wax funeral effigies of British monarchs, and a waxwork of Admiral Lord Nelson made specifically as a tourist attraction. There is also what is said to be the oldest stuffed parrot in the world – whose appearance certainly supports the claim.

There is a sense in which the magnificent Abbey itself (actually the Collegiate Church of St Peter) is a museum. Originally built by Edward the Confessor, rebuilt by Henry III, completed during 1376–1506 by Henry Yvele and others, the towers finished in 1734 by Hawksmoor, it has been the scene of the coronation of every British sovereign from William the Conqueror, and of the burial of Kings from Henry III to George II. Its harmonious architecture, its beautiful tombs and memorials of the royal and the famous, and its Royal Chapels (of which Henry VII's has been called 'the most beautiful in all Christendom') bring thousands upon thousands of visitors to stare rather than to worship.

Abbey open at all times – please respect services.
Museum *open 10.30–16.30 Mon–Sat. Charge.*
Royal Chapels *open 09.20–16.00 Mon–Fri; 09.20–14.00 & 16.00–17.00 Sat. Charge.*

SPECIALIST COLLECTIONS

All-Hallows-by-the-Tower 6 Q 32

Byward St EC3. 01-481 2928. The small 14thC crypt has a museum with a collection of Saxon crosses and Roman artefacts – and the only Roman mosaic floor in London which has not been resited. In fact it has lain here undisturbed since AD 122.

The church is interesting in its own right. It was founded in 675 and rebuilt during the 13th to 15th centuries. Second World War bombs made restoration necessary, including the addition of a new steeple, but the tower is still the one from which Pepys watched the Great Fire of London in 1666. Its memorial brasses, dating from the 14th to the 17th centuries, form the best collection in London (make an appointment before you get down to rubbing them) and its heraldic stained glass is very fine. By way of more modern interest, it is the guild church of the Toc H movement.

An unlooked for treat is the refectory, upstairs, which serves light lunches between *12.00 and 14.00 on weekdays. Open 09.00–17.30 Mon–Sun. Free.*

Bear Gardens Museum and Art Centre 6 O 28

Bear Gardens SE1. 01-928 6342. Elizabethan Bankside was a riotous assemblage of theatres, bear baiting gardens, inns and brothels which lay conveniently beyond the range of the law enforcers of the City of London. Its present-day landscaped riverside walks don't give much clue to its disreputable past – but the evocative and intriguing exhibitions in the museum do just that. Here are models of the *Globe* and other theatres, a diorama of the ice fairs held when the Thames froze solid, and an uninhibited look at the popular entertainment of 16thC and early 17thC Southwark riverside. There are occasional seasons of Shakespearean and other suitable live entertainments in the small replica of a 16thC playhouse, upstairs – phone or call for details. No refreshments, but the other side of the bridge (though the same side of the river) is the charming Anchor Inn, on the site of a disreputable earlier house which catered to the likes of those commemorated in the museum.
Open 10.30–17.30 Fri–Sun, Apr–Dec. Nat Hols 10.30–17.30. Feb–Mar by prior appointment only. Charge.

Bethnal Green Museum of Childhood

Cambridge Heath Rd E2. 01-980 2415. A particularly appealing branch of the Victoria and Albert Museum, with much material for those with serious interest in the social history of childhood. And much also for those with a more frivolous desire to peer into dozens of large and minutely equipped dolls' houses or to compare the facial expressions of Victorian with modern teddy bears!

The collection, on three light, airy, glass-roofed floors, which are currently being extended, consists of dolls and toys, dolls' houses, games, puppets and toy theatres, as well as a children's costume gallery, complete with nursery furniture and other bits and pieces associated with childhood. The rocking horses, toy trains, drumming mechanical

monkeys and kaleidoscopes have an instant appeal to – and there's no other way of saying it – children of all ages!
Children are welcomed in a most positive way, with *Saturday classes in the art room at 11.00 and 14.00* and workshops, activities and events during the Easter, summer and Christmas holidays. Even groups need not book, though school parties should book in with the Education Department of the V & A. Lavatories are to left and right immediately inside the main doors – sadly, there are no refreshments.
Open 10.00–18.00 Mon–Thu & Sat; 14.30–18.00 Sun. Closed Fri. Free.

British Crafts Centre   3 I 23
43 Earlham St WC2. 01-836 6993. Two floors giving a 'shop window' to the best of British craftwork. There are usually three or four exhibitions on at any one time – each featuring one craft through the work of three or four of its exponents. Most of the items are for sale. There's a coffee machine in case your throat gets dry in the company of all that wool and earthenware.
Open 10.00–17.30 Tue–Fri; 11.00–17.00 Sat. Closed Sun & Mon. Free.

Broadcasting Gallery   1 I 11
70 Brompton Rd SW3. 01-584 7011. Run by the Independent Broadcasting Authority, the gallery covers the story of independent radio and television. The guided tour, which lasts for 90 minutes, takes you through the whole story – showing how programmes are made, how advertising works, the technological progress in transmission and the importance of cable and satellite television. There are also cameras ancient and modern and models of some of the earliest sets.
Open by appointment only, Mon–Fri. Book for a tour at 10.00, 11.00, 14.00 or 15.00. Free. No children under 16.

Church Farm House Museum
Greyhound Hill, Hendon NW4. 01-203 0130. The 17thC gabled farmhouse still stands in its own tranquil garden although it no longer owns the surrounding fields from which it used to supply the London Hay Market. Downstairs the stone-floored kitchen with its huge fireplace is fully equipped with period pieces – pots, irons, jugs, a spit and a solid bake-oven. The dining room, whose panelling was originally in the bedrooms above, is informal and welcoming with its simple 18thC polished wood table, chairs and bookcase.
The front parlour and bedrooms are used for small changing

exhibitions of a quirky and appealing kind. Most popular are those on relatively recent local history, which tend to attract visitors above retirement age to exclaim over photographs of the area as they used to know it, and over artefacts still in use in their lifetimes. Of more general interest are the occasional arts and crafts exhibitions, which in the past have included paintings, drawings, stained glass work and tapestry.

Open 10.00–13.00 & 14.00–17.30 Mon–Sat (except Tue); Tue 10.00–13.00; Sun 14.00–17.30. Free.

Crafts Council Gallery   **5 J 20**
12 Waterloo Pl SW1. 01-930 4811. The Crafts Council is concerned with craft conservation and education and administers various grants and loan schemes to encourage new work. This administration goes on in No 8 – at No 12 a varied and changing exhibition programme is run. Here you may also acquire information and books and consult a well stocked colour slide index. There is a coffee bar for light refreshment and an in-house loo.

Open 10.00–17.00 Tue–Sat; 14.00–17.00 Sun. Closed Mon. Free.

Cuming Museum
Newington District Library, Walworth Rd SE17. 01-703 3324. The quaint and personal collection of Richard Cuming and his son, begun in 1872, to which has been added items of local and general interest disinterred from beneath Southwark during archaeological digs and the sinking of new foundations. The most obviously intriguing are on permanent display in the single large room. The rest come out in rotation in tiny special exhibitions – though they can be made available to students at virtually any time.

Always on show is the *Lovat collection of London superstitions* (mostly charms, and cures for rheumatism), an ironmonger's sign of a dog drinking from a pot which Dickens records having seen, the pump from the old Marshalsea Prison, an ex-dancing bear that is now stuffed and static, pilgrims badges and some nice, if severely chipped, late 12thC carvings from the Priory of St Mary Overie (now Southwark Cathedral).

Open 10.00–17.30 Tue–Sat; (19.00 Thu, 17.00 Sat); 14.00–17.00 Sun. Closed Mon & Nat Hols. Free.

Design Centre   **5 J 21**
28 Haymarket SW1. 01-839 8000. The Design Council (formerly the Council of Industrial Design) is an arbiter of

taste and quality, awarding its distinctive triangular marks of approval to British goods which come up to its high standards. Here you can see changing exhibitions of the newest of the approved. You can't buy (apart from a few smaller items like glassware and stationery) but a card index can point you to retail outlets. There's a coffee shop on the upper floor. Persevere if you want the loo, which exists but is tucked away.

Open 10.00–18.00 Mon & Tue; 10.00–20.00 Wed–Sat; 13.00–18.00 Sun. Free.

Foundling Hospital   **3 F 26**
(Thomas Coram Foundation for Children)
40 Brunswick Sq WC1. 01-278 2424. The charitable foundation, set up by a sea captain in the 18thC to give shelter to homeless children, now functions as an adoption and fostering agency and funds and supports research into all aspects of child care. Its premises have shrunk – the model in the central hall shows how much – but the outbuildings and colonnades can still be seen around the adjoining Coram's fields, a huge playground which adults may only enter if accompanied by a child.

The present relatively new building contains the original courtroom, reconstructed piece by piece, and a good collection of paintings, almost all by or of past governors. William Hogarth, an active member of the first Committee, presented his portrait of the founder and an untypical biblical scene of the bringing of the foundling Moses to Pharaoh's daughter. A third Hogarth was won in a raffle. Look out for the small circular Gainsborough of the Charterhouse; Handel's scores of his specially written *Foundling Hospital Anthem* and a version of the *Messiah*, and the mid-19thC series of pictures by Emma Brownlow of life at the hospital. (All the pictures in the background of her paintings are still on show today.) By the courtroom windows stand two cases of trinkets and coins left with children by destitute mothers. Social historians should ask to see the vellum-bound minute books, noting Hogarth's presence at so many meetings, and the bound sermons delivered over the years.

Open 10.00–16.00 Mon–Fri. Charge. Note: Sometimes closed for conferences, telephone first.

Geffrye Museum
Kingsland Rd E2. 01-739 8368. Named for a past Lord Mayor of London whose bequest founded the almshouses, built in 1715. The attractive low buildings, around a court of

towering planes, were converted into a museum of English furniture and woodwork early this century and opened in 1914. It is arranged as a series of fully furnished period rooms so that you can assess the development of design from Georgian England to the 1930s. (Unfortunately for dramatic effect, you have to retrace your steps to get out, as though the tape of time is running backwards). There are genuine shopfronts in the *Georgian street*, and a fully equipped open-hearth kitchen and woodworkers shop.

In the *Elizabethan room* note the 16thC linenfold panelling, carved chests and simple wrought-iron chandelier. The portraits give an idea of costume and you should imagine there are sweet herbs strewn on the floor.

The *Stuart room* has a ceiling which is a replica of the one in the *Master's Parlour* of the Pewterers Company Hall, rebuilt in 1668. Among the decorations you can pick out a master pewterer, St Catherine the patron saint and sea horses from the company's arms.

The *William and Mary room* has a fine black and gold English lacquer writing table and a pair of carved walnut chairs that only the quality would have sat upon.

The *Queen Anne room's* panelling is of c1700.

The simple *Chapel* is original, though most of the pews have been removed.

The *reference library and reading room*, created out of panelling from three separate houses of the 18thC has books, magazines and periodicals on open shelves, all relating to the decorative arts.

Behind it is the coffee shop – tiny and set in a corridor but light and welcoming.

The *early Georgian room* has pine panelling from Chancery Lane, mahogany furniture in the style of Chippendale, and Hubert van Kamp's only surviving spinet.

The *late Georgian room* has pine panelling from Aldgate, and furniture in the style of Heppelwhite.

In the *Regency room* note the rare William Frecker piano, the carved mahogany sofa resting on brass paws and the miniature sofa which may have been a craftsman's test piece.

The *mid-Victorian room* has Joseph Nash lithographs of the interior of the Great Exhibition and a walnut kneeling chair covered in Berlin woolwork among its characteristic clutter of furniture and ornaments.

Most of the items in the *Voysey room* were designed by Charles Voysey or his followers around the turn of the century, in a style which is a combination of English craftsmanship, à la William Morris, and Art Nouveau.

Bradmore House room. A bit of a time warp here. The house which once contained the room was built at Hammersmith by Thomas Archer in 1715.

The **exhibition hall** (the public lavatories are just behind it) mounts changing displays, often of costume.

The **1930s rooms** are upstairs – one an Art Deco suburban lounge of the mid 30s, the other a repository for the furniture of Gordon Russell Ltd, with Thomas C. Dugdale's moving painting of the *Arrival of the Jarrow Marchers in London*.

School visits are encouraged and projects and activities arranged in the holidays.

Open 10.00–17.00 Tue–Sat; 14.00–17.00 Sun. Closed Mon & Christmas. Free.

Goldsmith's Hall   6 L 29

Foster La EC2. For information, contact the City of London Information Centre on 01-606 3030. This classical-style palazzo, built in 1835 by Hardwick, opens its doors to the public once a month or thereabouts between October and July. The days vary because the reception rooms – which are as far as any visitor penetrates – are used for all manner of business functions. But if you take the trouble to book yourself in, on the number above, you will have a guided tour of as much of the unrivalled collection of antique plate (mostly silver-gilt) as the curator has seen fit to set out. And it'll be enough to dazzle you. Don't miss the showcases of modern gold jewellery you will pass near the staircase.

Open by appointment only. Charge.

Gunnersbury Park Museum

Gunnersbury Park, Pope's La W5. 01-992 1612. A branch of the Rothschild family used to live in this mansion, whose grounds are now a public park with a lakeful of water-fowl and a summertime café. The fine rooms, decorated in keeping with their marble columns and fireplaces, are used for a series of regularly changed exhibitions on local archaeology, history and topography. The transport collection of aged bikes and chariots and two smart Rothschild carriages is permanent, and so is the newly restored and correctly equipped Victorian kitchen. Research facilities are readily available for those interested in local studies, and the costume collection, if not on display, can be viewed on request.

On summer Sundays the Temple, a brief walk from the

house itself, is used for contemporary craft exhibitions by
day and for varied and popular concerts by night.
*Open 13.00–17.00 Mon–Fri; 14.00–18.00 Sat, Sun & Nat
Hols, Mar–Oct. 13.00–16.00 Mon–Fri; 14.00–16.00 Sat, Sun
& Nat Hols, Nov–Feb. Free.*

Horniman Museum
100 London Rd SE23. 01-699 2339. Given to the LCC, 'as
representing the people of London' in 1901 by Frederick
Horniman of the famous tea firm, the exhibitions are based
on his own personal collections of ethnography and natural
history. Though it has been enlarged, and is frequently
enriched with visiting exhibitions, it has retained that special
charm peculiar to such places. The building was designed by
C. Harrison Townsend in Art Nouveau style with a square-
based round-topped tower and an allegorical mosaic across
its front. The interior has an immediate appeal to children,
whose eyes light up at the skeletons and mummies, the
masks and stuffed tigers, and the first floor aquarium with
tree frogs and piranha fish and a working beehive at the
entrance.
Immediately inside the entrance are the lavatories, the
bookstall for guides and teaching worksheets, and entrances
to the library (*closed Mon*) and the lecture hall – for talks,
films and slide shows on all aspects of the museum. At the
far end of the south hall are the tea bar (*open 14.30–17.15
Mon–Fri & Sun; 11.00–17.15 Sat*) with stairs ahead (lined
with instruments of torture!) to the *aquarium* and stairs left
to the other galleries.
In general the *ethnographic collection*, covering the religious
beliefs and the arts and crafts of peoples from most parts of
the world, is in the ground floor south hall and south hall
balcony. The *natural history collection* is in the second floor
north hall and north hall balcony. And at the end of the
north hall is the *Dolmetsch collection of antique musical
instruments*.
Don't miss the park at the back where you may picnic, visit
the animal enclosure or launch into a nature trail.
*Open 10.30–18.00 Mon–Sat; 14.00–18.00 Sun. Closed Christ-
mas. Free.*

Jewish Museum　　　　　　　　　　　　　　　　3 E 25
Woburn House, Upper Woburn Pl WC1. 01-387 3081. A
small museum in an upstairs room of the Jewish Communal
Centre whose aim is to illustrate Jewish life, history and
religion. The largest single item is the 16thC Venetian ark at

the far end of the room. The screen beside it is used to show two audio-visual programmes on Jewish religion and ritual. Times of these vary and are often geared to visiting parties. The glass cases around the walls and down the centre of the room contain coins, a unique 7th or 8thC gold votive plaque with a Greek inscription, scrolls of the law, wood and silver containers for these, Torah mantles, Sabbath lamps, candlesticks, plate, pictures and everything necessary for the rite of circumcision. The curator, who is discovered immediately inside the door, is most informative about the collection and the purpose of the individual items.

Open 12.30–15.00 Mon–Thu, 10.30–12.45 Sun. Closed Fri, Sat, Nat & Jewish Hols. Free.

Kodak Museum

Headstone Dr, Harrow, Middx. 01-863 0534. Part of the earliest of the Kodak factories is the setting for a permanent exhibition on the art and craft of photography. First a small gallery for changing photographic exhibitions – then the showcases of the display proper.

This begins with before photography, showing miniatures and silhouettes and works its way through camera obscura, Daguerre's bright ideas and the contributions of Fox Talbot, Eastmann and others to the neat but less beguiling cameras of the late 20thC (from the warmth of early brass and wood to the cold silver and black of today).

The most unexpected items are the most appealing – the Victorian portable darkroom, the magic lanterns and shadow puppets, the detective and espionage cameras disguised as cigarette lighters and pens, and the mock-up of a Victorian photographic studio beside which a hidden tape offers the background sounds of horses, bells and the penetrating voice of a violet seller.

The audio-visual presentation – *A world of photography* – is easily unnerved by the many visitors and tends to switch itself off, so don't hold out too much hope for it.

Open 09.30–16.30 Mon–Fri; 14.00–18.00 Sat, Sun & Nat Hols. Free.

London Bible Gallery 6 M 28

The Bible Society, 146 Queen Victoria St EC4. 01-248 4751. The purpose of the Bible Society is the dissemination of the world's best seller. To this end they have initiated translations, including the 1976 *Good News Bible* (translated from English into English!) Their remarkable collection, displayed with the eager enthusiasm of a school project, is to be found in their library and down some spiral stairs in the crypt. There are 28,000 volumes, in 1,739 languages, the majority in glass-fronted library cases, but some laid out in showcases where their binding, illumination or unexpected scripts can be appreciated. There are miniature bibles that demand a magnifying glass, massive bibles that demand a lectern, the German bible of 1466, a Tahitian *Luke's Gospel* of 1818, John Eliot's Massachusetts *Indian New Testament* of 1661. There is a display on the history of the bible from the days of Hebrew and Greek to the most modern translation; a push-button quiz to test the knowledge of visiting children and three booths in which, by donning headphones, you can listen to readings in various languages.

Because the building is shared by other companies you must present yourself at the reception desk to be led upstairs. Guided tours can be arranged – otherwise they leave you to it. The route, marked with red arrows, ends in the bookshop – and no one wins a prize for guessing what's on sale.

Open 10.00–16.00 Mon–Fri. Closed Nat Hols & when new exhibition being set up. Free.

London Toy and Model Museum   **2 B 12**
23 Craven Hill W2. 01-262 8450/7905. This fascinating museum in a restored Victorian house is centred round two outstanding collections – the model train collection and the Victorian and Edwardian tin toy collection. On the ground floor, the Train Room displays a huge, historic selection of toy and model engines, carriages, rolling stock and stations from England, Europe, America and Japan.

In the Tin Toy Room are exquisite examples of toys ranging from the first motorcar to a space-age lunar module. Also on show are lead-flat toys, penny toys, fire-engines, buses and an 1875 riverboat by Marklin.

The Lower Galleries have three shops, one concentrating on Meccano products, an exhibition of toy animals and a nursery complete with bears, dolls and the cross-section of a furnished Victorian house. In the garden are two miniature working railways (electric and steam), a 56-seater bus for kiddie exploration and a café for refreshments. *Open Tue–Sat 10.00–17.30; Sun 11.00–17.00. Charge.*

Madame Tussaud's   **2 B 19**
Marylebone Rd NW1. 01-935 6861. Madame began her exhibition in Paris in 1770 with copies of the heads that fell from the guillotine. This – and the facsimile of herself showing a creepy little personage with steel-framed specs –

may account for the unsettling aura of this unique collection of wax effigies of the famous and notorious. First the fairytales and historical set-ups – Branwell Brontë painting his sisters, Sleeping Beauty despaired of by her doctor. Next the *Hall of heroes* where Elton John competes for attention with John McEnroe. Then the *conservatory* where the more extreme the original, the more realistic the model – Dame Edna Everidge and Barbara Cartland have startling impact. Later the *Royal hall of crowned heads and heads of state* standing or sitting in groups among which you may wander – (tourists photograph each other in apparent conversation with Harolds Wilson or Macmillan, Kings George I–VI.) Eventually, although you are offered an option of escape, you reach the simulated dungeon entrance to the *Chamber of Horrors*, advertised as Gothic fun but in fact genuinely gruesome, disturbing and unsuitable for young children. At last, if you have the stamina, you get to experience part of the Battle of Trafalgar from the gun deck of *Victory*, bangs, smoke, screams and all.

Cafeteria serves snacks and drinks under the beady eyes of a waxen family of Pearlies.

Open 10.00–18.00 Mon–Sun; closed 17.50 in winter. Charge. Special Royal Ticket includes admission to the Planetarium next door.

Martinware Pottery Collection

Southall Library, Osterley Park Rd Middx. 01-574 3412. Go upstairs to the reference library where a room has been set aside to display some of the work from the local Martinware Pottery. The bowls, heads and quizzically grotesque birds are heavy and distinctive and the Martin brothers, who worked in Southall from 1873 to 1923, guarded their techniques so jealously that there are no effective imitations. World-famous in a specialised sort of way.

Open 09.00–19.30 Tue, Thu & Fri; 09.00–16.45 Wed & Sat. Closed Mon & Nat Hols. Free.

Museum of Garden History   5 P 21

St Mary-at-Lambeth, Lambeth Palace Rd SE1. 01-373 4030. The pretty church, which was rebuilt in 1851 but still retains some 14thC features, was due for demolition in the 70s. It was rescued by the Tradescant Trust who turned it into a museum in memory of the two John Tradescants, father and son, buried with grandfather in the churchyard (next to Bligh of the Bounty). These two pioneering royal gardeners, who worked for Charles I and Henrietta Maria, travelled the world in search of new and unusual plants. Among the many they brought back were phlox and stocks and larch, Michaelmas daisies, plane trees and, of course, Tradescantia. They also made an extraordinary collection of rarities and curiosities – shells, stones, fossils, the American Indian cloak presented to Captain John Smith, desiccated fish, fowls and snakes. This material, after some dubious manoevring by Elias Ashmole, became the basis of the Ashmolean Museum in Oxford.

To work your way through the fascinating exhibition on their life and travels examine first the displays in the porch. Then enter the church and work your way around it, keeping the wall on your left. When you get back to the porch you can launch into the central displays and buy mugs, teatowels and books at the stall inside the door.

Don't miss out on the churchyard, currently being planted with examples of Tradescant imports. (And note that the two didn't have a monopoly on curiosities – in the 16thC a pedlar gave an acre of land to the church on condition that he and his dog had their own commemorative window, and there it is, on the south wall).

Open 11.00–15.00 Mon–Fri; 10.30–17.00 Sun. Closed Sat. Free but donation welcome.

Museum of the Order of St John   **3 I 29**

St John's Gate, St John's Sq EC1. 01-253 6644 Ext 35. First there were the Knights Hospitaller, a military order of crusaders who brought medical help to the wounded and to the sick among the pilgrims. Their base moved from the Holy Land to Cyprus and then to Malta, and meanwhile they were establishing themselves in other countries. The English order had its headquarters in the Priory of Clerkenwell from about 1140. The present Gatehouse, which is all that remains, was built quite late in the day in 1504. At the dissolution the order disappeared and did not resurface again until 1831. In 1837 the St John Ambulance Brigade was launched from the Gatehouse, and in 1882 the charitable St John Ophthalmic Hospital was founded in Jerusalem. In 1888 respectability was bestowed by Queen Victoria who made the order a British Royal Order of Chivalry with herself as sovereign at its head, a position the present Queen still holds.

The exhibition of missals, crosses, armour, documents and insignia in the one-roomed museum traces the history of the Order from its inception, in particular its connection with

Clerkenwell. Its most valuable possessions are two brilliantly painted panels from a 15thC Flemish altarpiece and the illuminated *Rhodes Missal*.

Don't miss out on a visit to the nearby St John's church (apply to curator for entry at the above number), restored above but with 12thC crypt. It has banners, paintings and two impressive tomb sculptures – an alabaster effigy of 1575 and an earlier figure of the last English Prior before the Reformation which makes no secret of the ravages of death.
Open 10.00–18.00 Tue, Fri & Sat. Closed Mon, Wed–Thu, Sun & Nat Hols. Free.

Musical Museum

368 High St, Brentford Middx. 01-560 8108. A small converted church holds – just – the immensely appealing collection of self-playing musical instruments amassed, cared for and demonstrated to visitors by the museum's founder and director, Frank Holland. Part of the charm of the place is that there is little attempt to make orderly displays of the player pianos, organs, orchestrions, orchestrelles, music boxes, barrel organs and the giant Wurlitzer. They are all crowded cheerfully together, with some 20,000 paper music rolls to operate them – many created from recordings by famous players. But the best part is that the instruments are not imprisoned in glass cages, the 90-minute guided tour (join in when you like) includes performances by most of them. They don't just sit there, they entertain as they should. Watch the keys of the Steinway depressed rhythmically, apparently by the ghostly fingers of Dame Myra Hess, as the sounds of her playing fill the church. And that's only the standard tour – a full concert is better still. Enquire for dates and booking facilities at the number above. Small, so large parties should book.
Open 14.00–17.00 Sat & Sun, Apr–Oct. Closed weekdays & winter. Charge.

National Museum of Labour History

Old Limehouse Town Hall, Commercial Rd E14. 01-515 3229. This exhibition has expanded from the single large room originally allocated to it and now fills much of the old town hall. Undoubtedly the most colourful and eye-catching aspect is its great banner display. For the rest, collect a guide sheet as you go in and work your way chronologically through the history of Socialism and the Trades Unions by way of documents, press cuttings, portraits, coins, medals, memorabilia and pictorial displays. There are also virtually continuous audio-visual presentations on people and events that have made their impact on the labour movement – Sylvia Pankhurst, for example, and the Industrial Revolution.

The museum is maintained by the Trade Union Labour Co-Operative and the Democratic History Society and behind the immediately accessible displays are research facilities and an extensive library. Talks are also arranged from time to time.

Open 09.30–17.00 Mon–Sat. Closed winter Nat Hols. Free.

Percival David Foundation of Chinese Art   **3 E 24**
53 Gordon Sq WC1. 01-387 3909. This highly specialised collection of exquisite Chinese porcelain from the Sung to the Ch'ing dynasties has recently been re-arranged. The ground floor gallery now holds a representative selection to serve as a 'taster' (or perhaps to satisfy the uninitiated who can only marvel at just so many fragile bowls and dragon emblems). The rest of the collection is set out in chronological order on the light and airy first and second floors. Detailed notes may be picked up in each room.
Open 14.00–17.00 Mon; 10.30–17.00 Tue–Fri; 10.30–13.00 Sat. Free.

Planetarium   **2 B 19**
Marylebone Rd NW1. 01-486 1121. In the *gallery of the astronomers*, models of scientists from Ptolemy to Einstein are trapped in transparent cages with the tools of their trade, while at regular intervals a voice-over enumerates their achievements, with special lighting effect accompaniment. Pass on through to the heart of the matter where reclining chairs encircle the amazing Zeiss, like some huge wise beetle, capable of projecting the night-sky – of any date and from any point on earth – onto the domed ceiling. Once an hour a deceptively reassuring voice will catapult your mind beyond the solar system and the galaxy and boggle it with stories of stars and space and the unconscionable scale of the cosmos. To take your mind off the unreasonable vastness of it all, book for a dazzling hour at a laser show in the adjoining Laserium (01-935 3726) *Wed–Sun evening. Open 11.00–16.30 Mon–Sun. Charge.* Special Royal Ticket includes admission to Tussaud's next door.

Pollocks Toy Museum   **2 F 22**
1 Scala St W1. 01-636 3452. Three rickety floors of small creaking rooms are packed with a magical mix of bygone toys. On the ground floor you may buy scale models and

Pollocks' own famous cut-out toy theatres. There are two stairways, each hung with intriguing displays, and you are directed up the one and down the other.

First floor, room 1: An Edwardian boys' den; optical toys, rocking horses and good old Meccano.

Second floor, room 2: Puppets hang around, but the main display is on Benjamin Pollock and the English Toy Theatre.

Third floor, room 3: Old and dignified wax and composition dolls – one of whom crossed the Rockies in the 19thC by covered wagon.

Third floor, room 4: Fierce little toy soldiers, ancient teddy bears, much mauled by love and time – and dolls' houses.

Second floor, room 5: Lots more dolls – china, rag, wood, celluloid, 'Pearly', clockwork, and a corner designed to look like a nursery of 1900.

First floor, room 6: More toy theatres, many set up for the performance of specific plays, the oldest dated 1820.

Open 10.00–17.00 Mon–Sat. Closed Sun & Nat Hols. Charge.

Prince Henry's Room   6 K 26
17 Fleet St EC4. 01-353 7323. One of the last remaining survivors of the Great Fire of 1666, the building was erected in 1610 as a tavern called the Prince's Arms. It is now thought to be a myth that the famous first floor room – the only one open to visitors – was designed for Prince Henry, eldest brother of Charles I, since the tavern's name was on record two years before he was born. Nevertheless, the fine Jacobean ceiling is decorated with the three feathers of the Prince of Wales and with the initials PH.

The room now contains a small exhibition of 'Pepysiana', on permanent loan from Samuel Pepys house at Brampton in Huntingdon, including contemporary pictures and views of London as it was when he wrote his famous diaries.

Open 13.45–17.00 Mon–Fri; 13.45–16.30 Sat. Closed mornings & Sun. Small charge.

Royal College of Music, Museum of Instruments   1 G 10
Prince Consort Rd SW7. 01-589 3643. First make an appointment – after that you will be guided to the exhibition, and round it if you wish. It has nearly 500 items on show – principally keyboard, wind and stringed instruments from the 16th to the 19th centuries, and including Handel's spinet. Note that the College's Department of Portraits is at the same address – see Art Galleries chapter.

Open term-time 10.30–16.30 Mon & Wed only. By appointment. Charge.

St Bride's Crypt Museum   **6 L 27**
St Bride's Church, Fleet St EC4. 01-353 1301. The Wren
church of 1670–84, whose distinctive spire has been the
inspiration for a million wedding cakes, has a museum of
excavated relics from Roman London to the present day,
found under or around it. The carefully revealed part-
Roman part-Saxon walls of the crypt itself contribute to the
reassuring coherence of the whole. The long and dramatic
history of London is easier to comprehend in the quiet of the
small but detailed exhibition. This is the printers' church –
and its warmth comes from the offices of Reuters, next
door.
Open 09.00–17.00 Mon–Sun. Free (donation appreciated).

St Paul's Crypt Museum   **6 M 28**
St Paul's Cathedral, Ludgate Hill EC4. 01-248 2705.
Europe's largest crypt has a rich *Treasury*, guarded by a pair
of enormous candlesticks, in which plate too valuable to be
used or stored in London churches is set out for the
admiration of the visitor in strictly secure showcases.
It features the plate of the Order of the British Empire,
whose chapel is down here, of the Order of St Michael and
St George, and of the Cathedral itself. You can also see
Wren's great model of St Paul's, the massive sarcophagi of
Nelson and the Duke of Wellington, and memorials to the
great – soldiers, artists, statesmen.
It would be a sin to leave without walking around the
Cathedral itself – Wren's greatest work and lasting monument – and itself a kind of art gallery. There are magnificent
stalls and organ casing by Grinling Gibbons, delicate ironwork by Tijou, vast paintings on the dome by Thornhill,
glittering mosaics by Salviati and Richmond, and a replica of
Holman Hunt's the *Light of the World*.
It is well worth the heart-pounding climb to the *Whispering
gallery*, not just to enjoy the weird phenomenon (words
whispered against one wall are audible on the opposite one)
but to get a different view of the whole.
*Open 10.00–15.15 Mon–Fri; 11.00–15.15 Sat. Closed Sun &
special service days. Charge.* Cathedral itself open at all
times – please respect services.

Sir John Soane's Museum   **3 I 25**
13 Lincoln's Inn Fields WC2. 01-405 2107. Sir John Soane
(1753–1837) was the eccentric and inventive neo-classical
architect whose masterpiece was the Bank of England. (This
was rebuilt in the 1920s, an event received sadly by all who

admire fine architecture). He adapted this house as a private residence and to hold his collection of architectural models, antiquities, books, plans and drawings – which also include original Piranesi drawings and most of the architectural drawings of the Adam brothers. The interior is so quirky yet so clever – with its cut away walls or floors and purpose-built niches – that you feel you are stepping into the man's own mind, its obsessive memory packed with all that fascinated him.

For the lay visitor the most immediately interesting items are the stone sarcophagus of Seti I, dated 1370 BC, which lies open and empty in the richly-filled basement, and the ante room displaying 12 paintings by Hogarth – the *Rake's Progress* and the *Election*. There are also works by Watteau, Canaletto, Turner and Reynolds and the extraordinary layout itself is intriguing even to those with no architectural knowledge at all.

Note that the books, plans and drawings are locked away in the more private reaches and only made available to those with an informed interest. That is, you should know what you want to see – don't expect to browse. Postcards and guides are on sale under the stairs, but for refreshments you'd better seek out Fleet Street and Strand to the south or High Holborn to the north.

Open 10.00–17.00 Tue–Sat. Closed Sun, Mon & Nat Hols. Free.

Tower of London 6 Q 32

Tower Hill EC3. 01-709 0765. This is London's oldest museum (the armouries have been inspiring awe in visitors since the days of the first Elizabeth) and the most popular. It was begun by William the Conqueror – the White Tower, or keep, was his – and has been added to by many of the sovereigns who followed. It has been one of the most impregnable fortresses in England, an arsenal and a prison. It is still designated a royal palace and was a royal residence until the time of James I. It has in its time housed the Royal Mint, the Public Records, the Royal Observatory and the Royal Menagerie. The many forcibly detained within it include the young Princess Elizabeth, Sir Walter Raleigh, Roger Casement and Rudolf Hess. Those beheaded on its green include Anne Boleyn, Catherine Howard and the 17-year-old Lady Jane Grey. Many more were taken from it to public execution on Tower Hill. Today it is guarded by Yeomen Warders and by six ravens, who are also on the nation's payroll on account of a legend that their departure will cause the whole edifice to topple.

To get your bearings, join one of the regular guided tours given by a Yeoman Warder (or Beefeater). Then regard the whole as a group of museums, all signposted from the parade ground. They are:

White Tower. Three floors and a basement of the largest and finest collection of medieval, 16th and 17thC and Tudor arms and armour in Britain. On the second floor is the simple Norman Chapel of St John, Britain's oldest church, still sanctified and still commanding respect.

Bloody Tower. Here two rooms are furnished as they might have been during the 12 years of Sir Walter Raleigh's imprisonment – quite comfortable, considering.

Beauchamp Tower. On the stairs and around the walls of the middle chamber are the intricately carved inscriptions by state prisoners – names, devices, monograms.

Bowyer Tower. Instruments of torture and the executioner's block and axe.

Oriental gallery and Herald's museum. In the former, elaborate armour for horse, elephant and samurai – so ferocious you'd as likely die from fear as from wounds. In the latter, coats of arms, banner devices and colourfully painted books of Arms.

History gallery. The story of the development of the Tower, in words, pictures and models.

Chapel Royal of St Peter Ad Vincula. Early 16thC with some illustrious though unmarked burials beneath its altar. Still in use – you may attend Sunday service on request at the Tower entrance.

Fusiliers' museum. Uniforms, models, silver, portraits of past Fusiliers and a case of Coalport porcelain. (*Small extra charge*).

Jewel House. Magnificent royal regalia from the 17thC (Oliver Cromwell did for the earlier stuff). Also the Crown Jewels and a great deal of royal plate. (*Extra charge*, and don't use a camera or the stringent security measures will clamp down on you).

It is now possible to walk almost all the way around the curtain wall of the inner ward, from the Wakefield to the Flint Tower, taking in the Salt Tower with its exhibition panels explaining the purpose of the towers; the Broad Arrow Tower which is arranged in the manner of a knight's apartments of 1381; and the Martin Tower from which Colonel Blood tried to steal the Crown Jewels in 1671.

There are no refreshments, but if you want to go out to eat and return, ask for a pass at the gate.
Open 09.30–17.00 Mon–Sat (16.00 in winter); 14.00–17.00 Sun. Closed Sun in winter & Nat Hols. Charge.

Wallace Collection   **2 D 18**

Hertford House, Manchester Sq W1. 01-935 0687. A magnificent collection of works of art amassed by the 3rd and 4th Marquesses of Hertford and by Sir Richard Wallace, illegitimate son of the 4th Marquess and heir to his possessions though not his title. It was bequeathed to the nation in 1897 by Lady Wallace under terms which preclude additions or loans, so that it retains a coherence and personality which national collections, however fine, lack. The lower rooms have the appearance of a lavishly furnished house – those above are galleries in which the works of art are more self-consciously displayed. Each repays careful attention, but don't miss the following –

Left from the entrance hall, through room 10, is room 9 and the shop.

1: Right of entrance hall. *18th and 19thC English pictures.* Hoppner's *Prince of Wales* has three feathers sprouting from its frame.

2: Left out of 1. *Ornate boulle furniture, 17thC European paintings and Sèvres porcelain.*

3: Back through 1 and straight ahead. Glimmering Limoges enamels, high relief miniatures under wraps in the centre cases, Venetian glass, medieval ecclesiastical art.

4: 15th–17thC objets d'art. Italian Renaissance bronzes, porcelain and earthenware.

Back corridor: Porcelain and earthenware and precious metals. And entrances to the marbled public lavatories.

5, 6, 7: Highly dramatic *European armour* for man and horse. Also arms, both highly decorated and highly aggressive.

8: Oriental arms and armour, including a Rajput warrior's coat-of-a-thousand-nails.

9: Guidebooks, postcards and two Landseers.

10: Paintings by Bonington and Delacroix. Leading off to the left, a corridor of Bonington and Turner watercolours.

11: Louis XIV furniture and pictures. (Francois Lemoyne committed suicide after completing *Time Revealing Truth*).

12: 18thC French decorative art. Two Oudry pictures of dead animals and a 19thC copy of an immense Louis XV desk. Go back to the entrance hall and up the grand staircase with its Louis XV balustrade and wall-covering Bouchers.

13: Canalettos and Guardis and Louis XV furniture.
14: Boulle furniture, Sèvres porcelain, more Canalettos.
15: 17thC Dutch, Flemish and Spanish paintings. A group of Rubens oil sketches, a Murillo, a Rembrandt.
16: 17thC Dutch genre paintings.
17: 17thC Dutch land and seascapes.
18: 17thC Dutch paintings with an Italian influence.
19: One of the world's great galleries. Here is Frans Hals' *Laughing Cavalier* in the illustrious company of Rembrandt, Velazquez, Rubens, Van Dyck, Poussin, Claude, Gainsborough, Reynolds, Romney and Lawrence.
20: 19thC French paintings.
21: 18thC French furniture and paintings. Watteau, Boucher, Fragonard and Greize. Also 16th–18thC miniatures in covered cases, including a portrait of Holbein.
22: Lady Wallace's bedroom. Principally Boucher, including his *Mme de Pompadour.*
23: 18thC English and French paintings.
24: Wallace's study. Decorative panels by Desportes and Oudry and boulle furniture.
25: Late 18thC French pictures, furniture and sculpture. And in almost every room is one or more elaborate and beautiful clock – in working order and primed to chime in close sequence rather than in vulgar chorus.
Open 10.00–17.00 Mon–Sat; 14.00–17.00 Sun. Closed Nat Hols. Free.

MUSIC AND DANCE ═══

British ballet is a relative newcomer. It didn't get off the ground, so to speak, until the founding of the Royal Academy of Dancing in 1920, followed within 10 years by Marie Rambert's Ballet Club and Ninette de Valois' company at Sadler's Wells in North London. British opera also was not born until Benjamin Britten's Peter Grimes was premiered in 1946. Yet now both have a world-wide reputation and London attracts top international singers, dancers and musicians to her opera houses and concert halls. And it is not only classical music that is well served – there is music of various kinds all over the place; church music, big bands pounding away in public parks, jazz and rock pouring out in pubs and clubs and halls – all combining to make London one of the richest and most exciting music centres in the world.

OPERA AND BALLET

Coliseum 5 J 22

St Martin's La WC2. 01-836 3161. The large and pleasantly gaudy theatre was built in 1902 for musical spectaculars, and, after a period of decline when it was given over to Cinerama, it became the home of the English National Opera, who always sing in English. Their varied and popular season lasts from Aug–May, with visiting companies filling in while the ENO disappears on summer tours. Subscribe to the 'Friends' scheme for priority booking, discounts and an entrée to dress rehearsals. There are also special offers for non-friends and treats like pre-performance talks and lunch-time concerts. Cold buffet service, coffee and drinks available from an hour before the performance – or reserve a supper table in the Dutch Bar or Terrace Bar (01-836 0111 Ext 114). The foyer bookstall is open all day.

Royal Opera House, Covent Garden 6 J 23

Floral St WC2. 01-240 1066. 24-hour recorded information on 01-240 1911. This splendid construction by E.M. Barry is the third theatre of the name on the site. It is home to the Royal Opera Company – founded as the Covent Garden Opera Company in 1946 – and the Royal Ballet Company who were based at Sadler's Wells until 1956. It is England's foremost opera house where you will see the great names of opera and ballet in a suitably lavish setting. The mailing list brings priority booking with discounts – or queue on the day for cheap amphitheatre tickets or the occasional sponsored prom performance. Cold buffets and drinks are served in all bars from one hour before the performance or order a light supper in the Crush Bar on 01-836 9453.

Sadler's Wells Theatre 3 G 30

Rosebery Av EC1. 01-278 8916. 24-hour recorded informa-tion 01-278 5450. Subscription and coach party hot line 01-278 0855. Once a spa – the original well discovered by Richard Sadler in 1683 is still there, under a trap door at the back of the stalls. This was the birthplace of both Royal Ballet companies and of the ENO, and is now the home of the English-singing New Sadler's Wells Opera and also the London base of the Sadler's Wells Royal Ballet (the touring one), and of visiting opera and dance companies. The mailing list brings information – become a Friend and you get newsletters, lectures and a chance to watch rehearsals as well. Work has begun on a small studio theatre, to adjoin, for community and educational events. There are bars and buffets for drinks and sandwiches – or order a salad meal on 01-278 6563 up to 15.00 on the day. The Sadler's Wells Stage Coach Service (an ordinary motor coach) will collect you from and return you to several major railway stations – enquire at the Box Office.

CONCERTS

Barbican Hall 6 K 30

Barbican Centre, EC2. 01-628 8795. The London Symphony Orchestra, whose base this is, offers three one-month-long seasons during the year. For the rest there is visiting opera, light classical music, jazz and even variety shows. See **Barbican Arts Centre** for fuller details.

Camden Centre 3 D26

Bidborough St, rear of Camden Town Hall WC1. 01-278 4444 Ext 2436. Hired out by Camden Council for multifarious events – including meetings, bazaars, opera and concerts of all kinds. Reopening early 1984 after redecoration.

Central Hall 5 M 19

Storeys Gate SW1. 01-222 6289. A conference centre in a listed building, in which the first meeting of the General Assembly of the United Nations took place in 1946. Is sometimes hired out for organ recitals and orchestral concerts.

Conway Hall 3 H 25

Red Lion Sq WC1. 01-242 8032. The building belongs to the South Place Ethical Society, a Humanist educational charity, which rents out its large and small halls for a programme of classical music from Sep–May, usually on Sun evenings. Tickets at the door.

Purcell Room 6 M 23

South Bank SE1. 01-928 3191. The smallest of the three South Bank concert halls, whose intimate atmosphere is ideal for chamber music and solo concerts. Bar and coffee bar in foyer, but see **Royal Festival Hall** for further facilities.

Queen Elizabeth Hall 6 M 23

South Bank SE1. 01-928 3191. Shares its foyer with the Purcell Room and uses its larger space for symphony, orchestral and big band concerts. Sometimes has special events such as film shows and Poetry International. See **Royal Festival Hall** for other facilities.

Royal Albert Hall 1 F 10

Kensington Gore SW7. 01-589 8212. Wonderful Victorian domed hall at the edge of the South Kensington museum complex. Perhaps best known for the summer 'Prom' concerts whose last night is traditionally awash with patriotic emotion. But all year round there are orchestral, choral and pop concerts, and even sporting events and large meetings. Bars for sandwiches and drinks.

Royal College of Music　　　　　　　　　　**1 G 10**
Prince Consort Rd SW7. 01-589 3643. Ask for a fixture list, published at the start of each term, to discover details of the chamber, orchestral and choral concerts and the operas put on by students in their opera theatre, concert hall and recital hall. Standards are high – also it's free. No refreshments (no space).

Royal Festival Hall　　　　　　　　　　**6 M 23**
South Bank SE1. 01-928 3191. Built for the Festival of Britain in 1951 and now part of the South Bank arts complex with the Purcell Room and Queen Elizabeth Hall, National Theatre, National Film Theatre and Hayward Gallery. Orchestral and choral concerts are staged in the 3,000 seat concert hall – and allow time to explore the foyers, open from noon daily, which always have at least one major exhibition as well as bars, a cafeteria and coffee bar, a wine and salad bar and a licensed restaurant – all pledged to feed you in time for the performance.

Royal Naval College
Greenwich SE10. Box Office 01-317 8687. There is a winter season of classical concerts in the beautiful Wren Chapel from Oct–Apr, and again during the two weeks of the Greenwich Festival in Jun. No refreshments, and although it is traditional to view the Painted Hall (Wren, painted by Thornhill) during the interval, you may not explore the rest of the College.

St John's　　　　　　　　　　**5 O 19**
Smith Square. SW1. 01-222 1061. 18thC church whose curious appearance has been likened to an upside-down footstool. Has regular lunchtime and evening concerts – solo recitals, chamber, orchestral and choral works. The crypt has exhibitions of works by contemporary artists and a good licensed buffet and restaurant. Become a Friend for privileged booking and discounts.

Wigmore Hall　　　　　　　　　　**2 E 19**
36 Wigmore St W1. 01-935 2141. An intimate atmosphere in which to hear chamber music, orchestral recitals and solo singers and instrumentalists. The best acoustics for guitar in London. The mailing list gives priority booking – and there are reductions if you take tickets for a season of five or more

Queen Elizabeth Hall, South Bank

concerts. In summer, book for a short Sun morning concert, starting at *11.30*, and enjoy a free sherry or coffee afterwards.

CHURCH MUSIC

The following churches usually have above average choirs or organists. They are Anglican unless otherwise stated (RC, Roman Catholic; B, Baptist; FC, Free Church).

All Hallows-by-the-Tower   **6 Q 32**
Byward St EC3. 01-481 2928. Founded 675 – Crypt Museum.
All Saints   **2 F 20**
Margaret St. W1. 01-636 9961. Gothic revival, 1859.
All Souls   **2 F 20**
Langham Pl. W1. 01-580 3522. John Nash, 1822–4.
Bloomsbury Central Church (B)   **2 I 21**
Shaftesbury Av WC2. 01-837 2102. John Gibson, 1845–8.
Brompton Oratory (RC)   **1 I 11**
Brompton Rd SW7. 01-589 4811. Italian Renaissance-style.
Central Hall Westminster (FC)   **5 M 19**
Storey's Gate SW1. 01-930 1801. French-style, concrete.

St Alban Holborn   3 I 27
Brooke St EC1. Mural by Hans Feilbusch.

St Botolph Aldgate   6 O 33
Aldgate High St EC3. 01-283 1670. Renatus Harris organ.

St Bride   6 L 27
Fleet Street EC4. 01-353 1301. Wren church with famous
spire.

St Giles Cripplegate   6 L 31
Fore St EC2. 01-606 3630. 14thC church within Barbican.

St James (RC)   2 D 18
Spanish Pl. W1. 01-935 0943. Early English style, 1895.

St Lawrence Jewry   6 M 30
Gresham St EC2. 01-600 9478. Wren church restored 1957.

St Martin-in-the-Fields   5 K 22
Trafalgar Square WC2. 01-930 1862. Also, lunchtime recitals
and concerts.

St Mary the Virgin   5 L 13
Bourne St SW1. 01-730 2423. Simple 1920s brick.

St Mary the Boltons   4 J 6
The Boltons SW10. By Godwin 1850; spire added later.

St Michael-upon-Cornhill (RC)   6 N 31
Cornhill EC3. 01-626 8841. Wren, but restored by Scott.

St Paul's Cathedral   6 M 28
EC4. 01-248 2705. Wren's crowning achievement.

Southwark Cathedral   6 Q 27
Borough High St SE1. 01-407 2939. 1206, but much restored.

The Temple Church   6 K 26
Inner Temple La EC4. 12thC round nave, 13thC choir.

Westminster Abbey   5 M 20
Broad Sanctuary SW1. 01-222 5152. Contains much of
Britain's royal history.

Westminster Cathedral (RC)   5 M 16
Ashley Pl SW1. 01-834 7452. Early Christian Byzantine
style, 1903.

LUNCHTIME MUSIC

Lunchtime concerts tend to be a feature of City churches
though are not exclusive to them. The following have regular
programmes – but see also the section on 'Open Air Music',
and on 'Rock and Jazz', because pubs sometimes have
lunchtime sessions, too.

All Hallows-by-the-Tower   6 Q 31
Byward St EC3. 01-481 2928. Classical hi-fi recordings at
13.00 on Mon and organ recitals at *12.15 and 13.15 on a Thu.*

Bishopsgate Institute 6 N 33

230 Bishopsgate EC2. 01-247 6844. Classical and chamber music at *13.05 on Tue* from Jan to end Apr and for a season in the autumn.

Holy Sepulchre 6 K28

Holborn Viaduct EC1. 01-248 1660. Vocal, instrumental or organ music at *13.15 on a Wed*, recorded music at the same time on *Tue and Fri* and a choral service at *13.20 on Thu.*

St Bride 6 L 27

Fleet St EC4. 01-353 1301. Organ recitals at *13.15 on a Wed.*

St John's 5 O 19

Smith Sq SW1. 01-222 1061. Solo recitals and chamber music *13.00 Mon and 13.15 alt Thu.*

St Lawrence Jewry 6 M 30

Gresham St EC2. 01-600 9478. Piano recitals *13.00 on Mon* and organ recitals *13.00 Tue.*

St Martin-in-the-Fields 5 K 22

Trafalgar Sq WC2. 01-930 0089. Concerts and vocalists at *13.05 Mon and Tue.*

St Mary-le-Bow 6 M 29

Cheapside EC2. 01-248 5139. Classical concerts at *13.05 on Thu.*

St Mary Woolnoth 6 N 30

Lombard St EC3. 01-626 9701. Church music is rehearsed from *13.05 on a Fri* by the 'singers workshop'. Visitors welcome.

St Michael-upon-Cornhill 6 N 31

Cornhill EC3. 01-626 8841. Organ recitals at *13.00 on Mon.* Also, worth getting the mailing list to catch up with the Elizabethan Singers, the 17thC Glee Club and the St Michael Singers who perform occasionally in the eve.

St Olave 6 P 32

Hart St. EC3. 01-488 4318. Classical recitals at *13.05 on Wed and Thu.*

St Paul's Cathedral 6 M 28

EC4. 01-248 4619. Organ recitals at *12.30 on Fri.*

Southwark Cathedral 6 Q 27

Borough High St SE1. 01-407 2939. Organ recitals at *1.10 on a Mon* – also choral recitals some evenings.

OPEN AIR MUSIC

In the summertime (generally between May and Sep) military bands offer free entertainment to office workers in City parks and squares, and those in the Royal parks flow over into Sun and Nat Hols. In the evenings there are

Bandstand, Hyde Park

symphony concerts and recitals in formal gardens and parks at which a seat or patch of grass may be booked for a small charge. Times and days vary somewhat – telephone first or check in *Time Out*, *What's On* or *City Limits*. Rain rarely stops play – this is Britain, after all.

Royal Parks Information on 01-211 3000. Military and brass bands play for free most lunchtimes.

Hyde Park, W2.	**2 H 15**
St James Park, SW1.	**5 L 19**
Regent's Park, NW1.	**2 B 21**

City Sites Information on 01-606 3030 (ask for City Information Centre). Or call in – it's in St Paul's Churchyard – to collect free leaflets on dates and times.

Finsbury Circus Gardens   **6 M 32**
Moorgate EC2. Lunchtime band concerts, usually *on Wed.*

Lincoln's Inn Fields   3 L 25

WC2. Military bands entertain legal London in its summer
lunch hours. Usually *Tue & Thu*.

Paternoster Square   6 L 28

EC4. Mostly military bands, sometimes the City of London
Girl Pipers. Get there early if you want to eat lunch at a
pavement café the while.

St Paul's Steps   6 M 28

EC4. Stroll or sit, in full view of St Paul's, for rousing
military band concerts. Usually *Thu*.

Tower Place   6 Q 31

EC3. The square is modern, the Tower and Thames are
venerable, the bands military, the day usually *Fri*.

Victoria Embankment Gardens   5 L 22

Riverside setting for military bands, massed bands and light
orchestras, most lunchtimes of the week.

Other sites

Alexandra Park

Wood Green N22. 01-444 7696. Band concerts in a sloping,
tree-planted park, usually at weekend lunchtimes.

Battersea Park   4 P 9

Concert Pavilion SW11. 01-633 1707. Lovely park, rich and
imaginative programme of musical events, lunchtime and
evening.

Crystal Palace Park

SE19. 01-633 1707. The Concert Bowl offers lakeside
symphony concerts *on Sun during Jul and Aug*. Book.

Greenwich Park

SE10. 01-211 3000. Military and brass bands *on Sun & Nat
Hols* at lunchtime and in the evening.

Holland Park   1 C 5

Court Theatre, W8. 01-633 1707. Near the romantically
melancholy remains of the Jacobean mansion, this small
open-air theatre offers a July programme of opera, ballet
and concerts. Booking not usually necessary.

Kenwood

Hampstead La NW3, 01-348 1286. Leading orchestras give
lakeside symphony concerts in a beautiful setting on *Sat
evenings during Jun and Jul*. Afficionados take a picnic.
There are also recitals in the elegant Orangery on *Sun
evenings* in spring and autumn. Book on 01-633 1707.

Parliament Hill

NW3. 01-485 4491. Lakeside setting for massed deck chairs
and massed bands on *summer Sat evenings*.

ROCK AND JAZZ

Britain, and specifically London, is the main centre for rock and jazz outside the USA. There is everything from major rock concerts and jazz club presentations of international stars to informal gigs in pubs which are cheap or even free. A selection of regular venues is listed below. Look in *Time Out*, *New Musical Express* or *Melody Maker* for information – and keep an eye, too, on the arts centres, the Lyric Hammersmith and even the concert halls which sometimes offer something unexpected and good.

The Jazz Centre Society at 35 Gt Russell St WC1 (01-580 8532) organises and promotes jazz concerts and has information on venues. But most importantly, it opens the National Jazz Centre in a converted warehouse at the above address at the end of 1983, with a performance space, shop, bar and restaurant. See musical press for details.

Bull's Head *Pub*

373 Lonsdale Rd SW13. 01-876 5241. One of the country's foremost jazz clubs in a Victorian pub overlooking the Thames. Modern jazz by top players nightly, with trad Sun lunchtimes. Real ale, and restaurant behind.

Dingwall's *Club*

Camden Lock, Chalk Farm Rd NW1. 01-267 4967. Barge-horse stables, near a busy weekend market, converted into a lively music club with burger-style restaurant. Mixture of rock, new wave and jazz funk from Mon–Sun evening with jazz at lunchtime on Sun.

Dominion *Theatre*   **3 G 23**

Tottenham Ct Rd W1. 01-580 9562. Huge cinema which stages seasons of live opera and rock concerts between the musical movies. Booking essential.

Greyhound *Pub*

175 Fulham Palace Rd W6. 01-385 0526. Old pub, purpose-built to stage live music – rock, new wave and reggae on Mon–Sat evenings. Snacks available.

Half Moon *Pub*

93 Lower Richmond Rd SW15. 01-788 2387. Big name bands belt out rock, jazz or pop in the large back room seven nights a week and Sun lunchtimes. Hot and cold food. Booking sometimes wise.

Hammersmith Odeon *Cinema*

Hammersmith Broadway W6. 01-748 4081. Large cinema entirely given over to live music – one night stands or seasons – often with internationally known names. Booking essential.

Kensington *Pub*   **1 B 3**
54 Russell Gdns W14. 01-603 3245. Every evening from
Mon–Sat two bands play, making this one of London's
leading rock venues. Snacks available.

King's Head *Pub*   **3 E 32**
115 Upper St N1. 01-226 1916. This famous and popular
theatre club has live rock and jazz after the show nightly –
about 22.00, or 20.00 on Sun.

Latchmere *Pub*   **4 R 6**
503 Battersea Pk Rd SW11. 01-228 4011. The fringe theatre
and restaurant arè upstairs, the rock, pop or 'novelty' gigs
are on the ground floor from Mon–Thu evenings, with jazz
at lunchtime on Sun. Bar snacks.

Marquee   **2 I 21**
90 Wardour St W1. 01-437 6603. One of the first of the
London rock clubs. No food, no membership, just good loud
music, *seven nights a week from 19.00.*

Maze *Club*   **2 H 22**
47 Frith St W1. 01-439 0747. Separate club above Ronnie
Scott's, with disco Mon–Thu evenings and live funk rock Fri
and Sat evenings. *Open 21.00–02.30. Closed Sun.*

New Golden Lion *Pub*   **4 L 4**
490 Fulham Rd SW6. 01-385 3942. Seven nights a week you
get rock, blues and R & B bands with a cabaret at lunchtime
on Sun. Cooked food always in adjoining **Whine Bah** (that's
what they call it).

New Merlin's Cave *Pub*   **3 G 29**
Margery St WC1. 01-837 2097. Barn-like pub with live rock,
reggae and jazz seven nights a week and a hot Sun lunchtime
session. Food at lunchtimes, real ale always.

100 Club   **2 G 22**
100 Oxford St W1. 01-636 0933. Room to dance and noisy
British jazz to make you want to, seven nights a week. Drinks
but no food. *Open 19.30–24.00, later Thu to Sat.*

Pegasus *Pub*
109 Green Lanes N16. 01-226 5930. Music fit to make a
horse fly, seven nights a week – jazz, R & B, reggae, rock,
Caribbean. No food.

Pizza Express *Restaurant*   **2 H 22**
10 Dean St W1. 01-439 8722. Jazz in the restaurant's
basement from Tue–Sun evenings.

Pizza on the Park *Restaurant*   **2 I 14**
11 Knightsbridge SW1. 01-235 5550. Jazz from Mon–Sat
evenings in the basement. Hamburgers as well as pizzas in
the restaurant.

Rock Garden *Restaurant*   **6 J 23**
6–7 The Piazza, Covent Gdn WC2. 01-240 3961. Lively
hamburger-and-chocolate-fudge-cake type of restaurant
with live rock played in its basement seven nights a week.
Ronnie Scott's   **2 H 22**
47 Frith St W1. 01-439 0747. The best jazz in London,
usually from major US jazzmen. Good food, subtle lighting,
comfort – but you'll need to book. *Open 20.30–03.00. Closed
Sun.*
Stanhope *Pub*   **1 I 7**
97 Gloucester Rd SW7. 01-373 4192. In the large upstairs
bar, groups play jazz, R & B and Latin American music
from Mon–Sat evening. Food always available.
Torrington *Pub*
4 Lodge La N12. 01-445 4710. Resident and visiting bands

play jazz-rock on Thu & Sun evenings in the restaurant which serves food at lunchtime only.

The Venue
160 Victoria St SW1. 01-834 5500. Converted cinema with large dance floor and plenty of tables and chairs for waitress service of food and drink. Sometimes taped music, sometimes top-name rock bands. *Open 19.30–03.00 Mon–Sat.*

Wembley Arena
Wembley Complex, Middx. 01-902 1234. Major rock concerts in the large arena which is part of the Wembley sports complex.

PHOTOGRAPHIC GALLERIES

Exhibitions of the photographer's art crop up from time to time in art galleries, museums and arts centres and these are detailed in the photographic press. The journal *Creative Camera* has reliable listings on its last page. However, the four galleries which follow can be relied upon always to have photographs on show.

Camerawork Gallery
121 Roman Rd E2. 01-980 6256. For the eyes of serious photographers – concerned mainly with social documentary work, photo-montage and exhibitions about questions of representation. You can usually get a good cup of coffee. *Open 13.00–18.00 Tue; 11.00–18.00 Wed–Sat; closed Mon. Free.*

Kodak Gallery   3 I 23
190 High Holborn WC1. 01-405 7841. Here you will find a series of changing exhibitions – each running about six weeks or so – which in their way cover most aspects of the art, from documentary pictures to business calendars. *Open 09.00–16.45 Mon–Fri; closed weekends and Nat Hols. Free.* There are changing exhibitions, too, at the Kodak Museum in Harrow, see 'Museums' chapter.

Light Fantastic   6 J 23
48 South Row, The Market, Covent Gdn WC2. 01-836 6423/4. Amongst the gift shops, street entertainers and cafés of the revamped Covent Garden Market is this small gallery

exhibiting and selling those curious three-dimensional pictures produced by laser-light and known as holograms. The latest, lightest and most fantastic aspect of photography. *Open 10.00–20.00 Mon–Sat; 12.00–18.00 Sun. Charge.*

Photographers' Gallery 5 J 22

8 Gt Newport St WC2. 01-836 7860. There's always an interesting and lively exhibition at No 8, and a good stock of photographic books and postcards to help you develop your interest. Two doors down at No 5 there is another gallery, a fascinating range of prints for sale and a small but civilised café-style coffee bar. *Open 11.00–19.00 Tue–Sat; closed Mon. Free.*

POETRY

London has a large number of small poetry groups, where established poets give readings or members read their own work and offer constructive criticism to each other. Poetry readings are also held from time to time in the large arts centres and in unexpected places like theatres and pubs. Main events of the week are in *Time Out*. For detailed lists of groups and workshops, evening classes, poetry magazines or specialist bookshops, send a s.a.e. to the Arts Council Poetry Library, 9 Long Acre WC2, stating which list you are after. Of the establishments below, the Poetry Society is the most generally important. The others are selected for their wideness of scope and regularity of meetings. There is usually an entry charge.

Camden Institute Poets

Haverstock Branch, Crogsland Rd, Chalk Farm NW1. 01-485 9023. Meet on *Mon evenings* in term-time for readings and discussions of contemporary poetry, followed by a workshop for members to air their own. *Charge.*

City Lit J I 24

Stukeley St, Drury La WC2. 01-242 9872. Runs day and evening classes on contemporary poetry, verse speaking, and the writing of poetry. Telephone first for current information. *Fees payable per term.*

National Sound Archive 1 H 10

British Institute of Recorded Sound, 29 Exhibition Rd SW7.

01-589 6603. This is where to go for the strange and impressive experience of hearing Tennyson and Browning reading their own works. Also other writers, both living and dead. Appointment wise. *Open 10.30–17.30 Mon–Fri; to 21.00 Thu.*

Pentameters
Three Horseshoes Pub, Heath St, Hampstead NW3. 01-435 3648. Arranges readings by distinguished poets at fairly regular intervals. Occasionally falls into fallow periods so check here or with the Poetry Library or Poetry Society.

Poetry Society   1 H 5
21 Earl's Court Sq SW5. 01-373 7861. New and established poets appear in its quarterly Poetry Review, and its book-shop sells magazines, anthologies, criticism and do-it-your-self advice for aspiring poets (by mail order if you wish). Holds twice weekly readings by well-known poets on *Tue and Thu evenings*. On *Wed evening* the theatre is used by the workshop Poetry Rounds. Sometimes arranges one-off events outside its own premises. Open to non-members, though membership brings discounts and regular informa-tion. *Open 09.30–17.00 Mon–Fri and during events evenings. Closed weekends.*

Stratford Poets
Tom Allen Club, Grove Crescent Rd, Stratford E15. Contact: 01-534 4545 Extn 421. The Newnham Arts Council poetry workshop for reading and discussing the work of members and of established poets. *Meet fortnightly on a Mon evening.*

Troubadour Poets   1 I 7
Troubadour Coffee House, 265 Old Brompton Rd SW5. Contact: 01-499 4080 Extn 280. Live music and live poetry on *Mon evening* in a relaxed coffee house atmosphere. Hot chocolate is recommended.

THEATRE ═══════════════

The tradition of live theatre in London has flourished – give or take the odd setback caused by war, pestilence or inflation – since 1576 when the round wooden Theatre was built south of the Thames (predating Shakespeare's Globe by 22 years). More than 400 years later there are 37 commercial West End theatres. There are also two major subsidised companies, the National Theatre on the South Bank and the Royal Shakespeare Company which moved from the Aldwych to the Barbican in 1982. Both operate mailing list schemes which give early booking opportunities. Performance details of all theatres appear in the national press, *Time Out* and *City Limits*. Seats may be booked at each theatre's own box office or through a ticket agency, though the latter will charge a fee. For 'last minute orders' go to the half-price ticket office in Leicester Square, a green and yellow chalet opposite the Swiss Centre, *open 14.30–18.30 Mon–Sat and also 12.00–14.00 on matinee days*. Tickets are for that day only – no credit cards, no cheques, no seating plans, no nonsense.

For the adventurous, so-called fringe or alternative theatre is among the liveliest and most exciting in the world. New approaches and new departures often have their beginnings in the informal atmosphere of converted halls and the back rooms of pubs. Almost all are clubs but membership is readily available at the door. Some run mailing lists, all advertise in *Time Out*, and though each has its own box office there is a central fringe booking office in the foyer of the Criterion Theatre, Piccadilly, 01-839 6987.

WEST END THEATRES

Adelphi, Strand WC2. 01-836 7611.
Albery, St Martin's La WC2. 01-836 3878.
Aldwych, Aldwych WC2. 01-836 6404/01-379 6233.
Ambassadors, West St, Cambridge Circus WC2. 01-836 1171.
Apollo, Shaftesbury Av W1. 01-437 2663.
Apollo Victoria, 17 Wilton Rd SW1. 01-828 8665.
Astoria, Charing Cross Rd WC2. 01-437 6565.
Comedy, Panton St SW1. 01-930 2578.
Criterion, Piccadilly Circus W1. 01-930 3216.
Drury Lane (Theatre Royal) Drury La WC2. 01-836 8108.
Duchess, Catherine St WC2. 01-836 8243.
Duke of York's, St Martin's La, WC2. 01-836 5122.
Fortune, Russell St WC2. 01-836 2238.
Garrick, Charing Cross Rd WC2. 01-836 4601.
Globe, Shaftesbury Av W1. 01-437 1592.
Haymarket, (Theatre Royal) Haymarket W1. 01-930 9832.
Her Majesty's, Haymarket SW1. 01-930 6606.
Lyric, Shaftesbury Av W1. 01-437 3686.
Mayfair, Stratton St W1. 01-629 3036.

National Theatre, South Bank SE1. 01-928 2252.
New London, Drury La WC2. 01-405 0072.
Old Vic, Waterloo Rd SE1. 01-928 7616.
Palace, Shaftesbury Av W1. 01-437 6834.
Palladium, Argyll St W1. 01-437 7373/2055.
Phoenix, Charing Cross Rd WC2. 01-836 2294.
Piccadilly, Denman St W1. 01-437 4506.
Prince Edward, Old Compton St W1. 01-437 6877.
Prince of Wales, Coventry St W1. 01-930 8681.
Queen's, Shaftesbury Av W1. 01-734 1166.
St Martin's, West St, Cambridge Circus WC2. 01-836 1443.
Savoy, Strand WC2. 01-836 8888.
Shaftesbury, Shaftesbury Av WC2. 01-836 6596.
Strand, Aldwych WC2. 01-836 2660/4143.
Vaudeville, Strand WC2. 01-836 9988.
Victoria Palace, Victoria St SW1. 01-834 1317/8.
Westminster, Palace St SW1. 01-834 0283.
Wyndham's, Charing Cross Rd WC2. 01-836 3028.

FAMOUS THEATRES

Criterion   **2 I 18**
Piccadilly Circus W1. 01-930 3216. A listed building, which
also deserves mention as London's only underground
theatre – in the strictly physical sense. You even go down to
the Upper Circle, through a lobby still decorated with the
original Victorian tiles. Here, too, a separate box office – 01-
839 6987 – handles bookings for all current fringe and
experimental theatrical productions in London.

Garrick   **2 I 22**
Charing Cross Rd WC2. 01-836 4601. Virtually unchanged
since it was completed in 1889 (after a struggle with an
underground river, forgotten since Roman times, which
tried to flood the foundations). Bourchier and Jack Bucha-
nan once put on shows here. Varied bills these days.

Lyric, Hammersmith
King St W6. 01-741 2311. A short step from Hammersmith
tube station are four floors of theatre, music and exhibitions.
Box office at ground level; studio theatre, bar and wine-bar-
style restaurant on first floor; entrances to theatre, with
sumptuous recreation of a Victorian auditorium, on second
and third floors, each with foyer and bar or coffee bar.
Productions range through classic, modern and fringe. Jazz
in the foyer Sat lunchtime; concerts occasional Fri lunchtimes; crafts fair Sat morning; regular exhibitions of paint-

ings and prints. Call in any time for a drink or snack or to see what gives. *Open 10.00–23.00 Mon–Sat. Closed Sun.*

National Theatre   **6 M 23**
South Bank SE1. 01-928 2252. Britain's National Theatre can be found in the massive concrete structure between Hungerford and Waterloo bridges, known as the South Bank complex. It may be a little short of beautiful from the outside. But on its tree-lined riverside walks, its jutting terraces, and in its foyer bars with their huge windows, the views are stunning. To the far right stands St Paul's, to the left the Houses of Parliament, and after dark lights glitter on the water.
World-famous for its first-class productions of new, classic, foreign and experimental plays. There are three theatres, the large Olivier with its open thrust stage; the smaller Lyttleton with its proscenium arch and the adaptable little Cottesloe for experimental productions. Book on 01-928 2252. A few seats are held back for sale to personal callers from *10.00* on the day of the performance. Mailing list (charge) brings priority booking opportunities.
All the theatres share the same facilities. The National Theatre Restaurant, 01-928 2033, Ext 531, serves full dinners *from 17.30–01.00*. The Lyttleton Buffet is a self-service snack bar, *open 10.00–23.00*. There are bars and coffee bars on every floor, *open pub hours and 10.00–23.00 respectively*, and there is no need to have a ticket for the theatre to enjoy them. Theatre and art books are on sale in the Lyttleton foyer bookshop *from 10.00–23.00* and also outside the Olivier stalls for two hours before each performance. The art gallery on the top floor has changing exhibitions, exhibitions sometimes appear in the foyers, and there is usually live music in the Lyttleton foyer in the early evening, all free. You can even have a free tour of the whole building, including backstage – book on 01-633 0880.

Palladium   **2 G 20**
8 Argyll St W1. 01-437 7373. Variety shows par excellence, international names, a panto every Christmas and all the glitter of the Royal Command Performance.

Old Vic   **6 O 24**
Waterloo Rd SE1. 01-928 7616. Built in 1818, taken over in 1912 by the inimitable Lilian Baylis, who for many years used it to present opera, concerts, drama and especially Shakespeare at reasonable prices. The home of the National Theatre Company from '62 to '76, then of the Prospect

Theatre Company, this theatrical monument found itself up for sale in 1982. The eventual Canadian purchaser has recreated the late Victorian decor for the reopening in autumn 1983, hopefully for a future as successful as its famous past.

Royal Shakespeare Company
Barbican Theatre, Barbican Centre EC2. 01-628 8795. The RSC, which is based at Stratford-upon-Avon, is Britain's leading subsidised company. Apart from regular presentations of Shakespeare's plays it presents new plays, revivals and ambitious experimental productions – for example, the works of Harold Pinter, and David Mercer, a revival of *Wild Oats* and the ambitious and highly successful version of *Nicholas Nickleby*.

The company's London base is at the Barbican Centre (see page 22), and has at its disposal the large, purpose-built main theatre and, beneath it, the small studio theatre, the Pit.

Savoy   6 K 23
Strand WC2. 01-836 8888. Built by Richard D'Oyly Carte as a home for the comic operas of Gilbert and Sullivan, and the first public building in the world to be blessed with electric light. Now presents a variety of plays and musicals. Attached to the Savoy Hotel with its famous Grill Room, restaurants and bars.

National Theatre, South Bank

Shaftesbury   2 I 21
Shaftesbury Av WC2. 01-836 6596. Was acquired in the
spring of 1983, by a company of some of the best of British
comedy actors, and is now a Theatre of Comedy of all sorts –
classical and modern, farcical and sophisticated.

Theatre Royal, Drury Lane   6 J 24
Catherine St WC2. 01-836 8108. The glamorous, richly
decorated successor to three earlier theatres on the site
(generally referred to as 'Drury Lane'). The royal box has
seated every British sovereign since Charles II. Famous for
lavish musicals – *Oklahoma*, *My Fair Lady*, *A Chorus Line* –
and for the man in grey, best-loved of theatre ghosts.

Theatre Royal, Haymarket   5 J 21
Haymarket SW1. 01-930 9832. Founded early in the 18thC
as 'the little theatre in the Hay', this one has come a long
way, especially since it moved into the present building in
the 1820s. Plays of quality are presented here, as befits the
grand Palladian Nash exterior and the gracious, gilded
interior.

Vaudeville   6 K 23
Strand WC2. 01-836 9988. What you have here now is
primarily straight theatre in an attractive listed building. But
the name comes from earlier times when music hall and
burlesque roistered away within its walls.

FRINGE AND PUB THEATRE

Arts Theatre Club   2 I 22
6 Gt Newport St WC2. 01-836 2132. Opened in 1927 as a
club theatre to circumvent the Lord Chamberlain's censori-
ous restrictions. Nowadays the Arts Club itself is separate
from the two theatres, one small and one a studio, which
offer experimental plays. Tom Stoppard's *Dirty Linen* and
Newfoundland here became the longest-running fringe
double-bill of all time. Here, too, the Unicorn Theatre puts
on children's plays for schools with public matinees on Sat
and Sun. Lounge bar on the ground floor, snack bar above.

Bloomsbury Theatre   3 D 24
15 Gordon St WC1. 01-387 9629. Used in the winter half of
the year primarily by the student societies of the University
of London, and for the summer half and at Christmas by
professional touring companies who bring opera, ballet and
drama to its stage. There are frequent lunchtime concerts of

classical, jazz and rock music and the occasional short film season. The bar and the coffee and snack bar open an hour before performances.

Bridge Lane Theatre   4 P 6
Bridge La SW11. 01-228 5185. One of the most recent of fringe venues, which achieved critical acclaim and expansion within its first year. Professional resident and visiting companies offer new or neglected plays and children's holiday matinees. A new scheme of summer workshops in dance and drama, with the use of video, is planned. Café and bar to sustain you before and after.

Bull and Gate
389 Kentish Town Rd NW5. 01-485 0274. The Hampstead Theatre Club offers plays, or cabarets with sociological claws, in an annexe at the back from *Tue–Sat*. Membership waived for those with local library tickets. Hot and cold snacks and real ales on tap in the pub.

Bush Theatre
Bush Hotel, Shepherd's Bush Green W12. 01-743 3388. Above the large and busy pub, and originally established to appeal to non-theatre-goers, its exciting and varied new productions not infrequently transfer to the West End. *Performances from Tue to Sat.*

Café Theatre Upstairs   2 I 22
Bear and Staff Pub, 37 Charing Cross Rd WC1. 01-240 0794.

Café Theatre Studio   2 I 22
De Hems Pub, Macclesfield St W1. 01-240 0794. Both are run by the Artaud Theatre Company who create an amazing flow of entertainment with a minimum of one lunch-time and two evening shows in each small theatre. New plays, modern classics and adaptations of novels and stories come to life from *Mon to Sat*. Sometimes they even throw in a poetry reading on *Sun*. You may take snacks or drinks from the bar into the theatre with you.

Donmar Warehouse   3 I 23
41 Earlham St WC2. 01-836 1071. This studio theatre is a lot classier and more comfortable than it was in the days when the Royal Shakespeare Company used it for experimental productions. It welcomes touring companies, mounts its own productions and is a mixture of fringe venue and small legitimate West End Theatre.

Drill Hall   3 F 23
16 Chenies St WC1. 01-637 8270. The plentiful spaces of the
ex-Territorial Army drill hall are used in a variety of ways –
as rehearsal rooms, for lunchtime and evening classes and
dance workshops, (complete with crèche), and to accommodate a bar and basement Soup Kitchen which serves snacks
of a stoneground and natural kind from *11.00 until the start
of the evening performance Mon–Fri*, and for an hour before
the performance at weekends. But the core of the place is its
performance space where travelling fringe theatre, alternative cabaret, opera and music draw enthusiastic audiences.

Finborough Arms   4 J 5
118 Finborough Rd SW10. 01-373 2631. The resident Good
Company offers new plays, some by the resident writer,
though new scripts with local relevance are always con-
sidered. Stay after the show on *Fri* and *Sat* for alternative
cabaret. Tasty bar snacks. *Evening theatre only*.

Gate Theatre at the Latchmere   4 R 6
503 Battersea Park Rd SW11. 01-228 2620. Opened in 1982,
above a real-ale pub, this one has already established a good
reputation. There is a cocktail bar and an enterprising
restaurant on the same floor. *Performances Mon–Sat evenings only*.

Gate Theatre at the Prince Albert   1 A 8
11 Pembridge Rd W11. 01-229 0706. Older brother of the
venture above and, like it, specialising in new plays and the
lesser known works of important writers. Pub below will
quench your thirst but not feed you. *Performances Mon–Sat,
evenings only*.

Greenwich Theatre
Crooms Hill SE10. 01-858 7755. Purpose-built with a large
ground floor restaurant, *open 12.00–15.00 and 18.00 until
after the show*, which has a bar in one corner and a wine bar
in the other. Upstairs a light, airy space houses changing
exhibitions of paintings, frequently by local and established
artists. The theatre itself mounts a season of seven plays a
year – new ones, revivals and classics – often with famous
names in the cast list (Glenda Jackson, Susannah York, Tom
Courtenay for example).

Grove Theatre
Grove Tavern, 83 Hammersmith Gro W6. 01-748 2966.
Studio theatre above a pub, offering a mixture of foreign

works in translation and new plays, making what they hope is their London debut. *Performances Tue–Sun evenings only.*

Hampstead Theatre Club

Swiss Cottage Centre, Avenue Rd NW3. 01-722 9301. One of the leading club theatres, which has acquired a respectability at variance with its controversial and experimental productions. Responsible for giving Michael Frayn's *Clouds* and *Alphabetical Order* and Pam Gems' *Dusa, Fish, Stas and Vi* to the West End and Mike Leigh's brilliant improvisations both to the West End and to television. Licensed bar and coffee bar.

Jeanetta Cochrane Theatre   3 H 25

Southampton Row WC1. 01-242 7040. Built for the Central School of Art and Design and named for one of its early costume designers. During vacations the Ballet Rambert, National Youth Theatre, Children's Music Theatre and the Theatre of the Deaf display their talents. Nothing headier to drink than orange squash.

King's Head   3 D 33

115 Upper St N1. 01-225 1916. Arguably the best-known and most widely reviewed of pub theatres, presenting musicals, reviews, new plays, revivals. There are two kinds of ticket, for performance only, or for a meal as well, in which case you watch the show from your table. The pub itself has live music seven nights a week. *Theatre Mon–Sat, lunchtime and evening.*

Mermaid   6 M 27

Puddle Dock, Blackfriars EC4. 01-236 5568. Lord Bernard Miles' creation, established in the late 50s as an Elizabethan-style theatre across the River from the site of Shakespeare's Globe. Renovated and reopened in 1981 with a restaurant and two bars overlooking the Thames, this is a friendly and welcoming setting for new plays, revivals, musicals, riotous Christmas shows and the Molecule Club children's theatre.

New Half Moon

213 Mile End Rd E1. 01-790 4000. Has a national, indeed international, reputation for popular plays, not always radical, but also has strong community links. 1984 should see the opening of its new building with space for workshops, a bar and restaurant, which it is hoped will make it a focal point for the area.

New Inn

St Mary's Rd W5. 01-567 8352. Studio theatre above an appealingly Dickensian pub (good food at lunchtime but none in the evening). Shows mostly one-act plays by established writers, put on by visiting companies, though revues and music hall are not unknown.

Old Red Lion   **6 J 29**

418 St John St EC1. 01-837 7816. Lunchtime and evening performances of a mixed bag of plays presented by the resident company with professionals brought in from outside if necessary. The pub, which stands on a right of way and used to be known as 'the in and out at the Angel' has good food at all times.

Orange Tree

45 Kew Rd, Richmond Surrey. 01-940 3633. Attractive and classy early Victorian pub. The comfortable cellar restaurant serves European food at reasonable prices. The highly successful theatre upstairs stages plays principally by well-known contemporary writers – Fay Weldon, Tom Stoppard, David Halliwell. There is a 'Kids Festival' in August and occasional outdoor productions in summer. *Theatre Mon–Sat, lunchtime May–Aug; evening Sep–Apr.*

Pindar of Wakefield   **3 G 27**

328 Gray's Inn Rd WC1. 01-837 7269. This ancient inn is now the home of the AbaDaba Music Hall which hires professional actors to present lively, sometimes bawdy, modern music-hall, pantomime and sing-songs. Crowded enough to make booking essential – ring the pub, or the company itself on 01-722 5395. Basket meals are available while you watch. *Theatre Thu–Sat.*

Players Theatre Club   **5 K 22**

Villiers St WC2. 01-839 1134. The Victorian music-hall is alive and well and presenting for your delectation rollicking frolicsome festivities of a hilarious and multifarious nature. There are two bars and a supper room, and drinks and sandwiches are served during the performance. (Even temporary membership must be taken out in person, 48 hours before the show.)

Royal Court   **5 L 12**

Sloane Sq SW1. 01-730 1745. Renowned avant-garde theatre which amazed its public at the beginning of the century with works by George Bernard Shaw and launched a whole new wave of drama in the late 50s with John Osborne's *Look Back in Anger*. Still stages experimental work by modern writers. Has a snack bar, two bars and a bookstall. In the studio Theatre Upstairs – 01-730 2554 – the Young People's Theatre Scheme puts on annual festivals of new plays and there are also rehearsed readings of previously untried scripts.

St George's Elizabethan Theatre
49 Tufnell Park Rd N7. 01-607 1128. This unusual octagonal theatre with a thrust stage and no proscenium is a replica of an Elizabethan theatre. Predominantly Elizabethan productions *from Thu–Sat evening and in matinee the rest of the week* when it is packed with school parties. Sometimes holds jazz concerts or poetry recitals on a Sun. Foyer vegetarian buffet is *open 10.00–24.00* – all welcome. Bars open usual hours.

Shaw Theatre   **3 D 26**
100 Euston Rd NW1. 01-388 1394. Camden Council's community theatre and the permanent home of the New Shaw Theatre Company. Varied programme of straight plays, musicals, concerts, mime, dance and children's events catering for both minority and majority tastes. Stages a lavish Christmas pantomime and features a summer season by the National Youth Theatre. Regular lunchtime concerts in the bar.

Soho Poly Theatre Club   **2 F 21**
16 Riding House St W1. 01-636 9050. Entirely geared to launching new, hitherto unproduced work by new writers, many of whom have amply justified its faith. Small basement performance space; ground floor foyer serves soup, bread and cheese, coffee – and hopes for a bar licence.

The Swan
17 Needham Rd W11. 01-328 8838. The theatre above this welcoming, neighbourhood pub is the permanent home of the Wet Paint Theatre Company. Described as 'Britain's only punk theatre group', the company specialise in plays by Chris Ward. Changing programme attracts a young audience. *Usually Tue–Sun eve.*

Theatre Royal, Stratford East
Gerry Raffles Sq E15. 01-534 0310. Joan Littlewood's brainchild is fighting a winning battle against financial problems. It offers drama, variety, Christmas pantomimes and Sun concerts in its main and studio theatres and rehearsed play readings of productions too expensive to stage. It also busies itself in the community, initiating

projects and co-operating with schools in the use of drama as a teaching aid. Bar and snack bar open before the show. *Theatre closed Mon.*

Tramshed
ABC Picture House, Wellington St SE18. 01-855 3371. Born in the nearby converted tramshed, the company has just moved to more and better facilities in the old cinema. It intends to maintain its reputation as a lively venue for travelling fringe theatre, cabaret, feminist revue and live music. Snack bar and bar.

Tricycle Theatre
269 Kilburn High Rd NW6. 01-328 8626. A shop window for new drama – both in-house and incoming productions – with *evening shows from Mon to Sat, a kids matinee before the regular Sat mat*, and occasional Sunday specials of dance or music. The foyer bar, with its coffee, snacks, and real ale in licensing hours, is *open from 10.00–22.30* and much loved as a 'local' by those who live nearby.

Young Vic   6 O 24
66 The Cut SE1. 01-928 6363. Established as a young people's repertoire theatre with the emphasis on the classics and established modern plays. When the Young Vic Company is touring, the Royal Shakespeare Company and the Ballet Rambert visit. Café-style vegetarian restaurant open at lunchtime and before the show. If overcrowded there is a pub, a licensed café and a good restaurant to hand.

CHILDREN'S THEATRE
Little Angel   3 D 33
14 Dagmar Passage, Cross St N1. 01-226 1787. London's only permanent marionette theatre (they're the puppets with strings). Excellent shows, at weekends and in the school holidays, by the resident company and visiting puppeteers. Essential to book – disappointed children are no fun to be with.

Polka Children's Theatre
240 The Broadway, Wimbledon SW19. 01-543 4888. Well worth the trek out of town to this bright and lively centre whose shows often involve mime, puppets, masks, clowns and noisy audience participation. There is also a magical exhibition of toys and puppets, a small playground with slides etc, workshops and classes for adults and children in arts and crafts – and the Polka Pantry for chocolate cake, orange juice, ice cream and other messy treats.

Unicorn Theatre 2 I 22
Gt Newport St WC2. Box office 01-836 3334. Unicorn club
01-379 3280. Presents an extensive programme of new and
classic plays specially suited for children within the four to 12
age group. Puppet shows, conjurors, mime shows and
concerts are included in the varied repertoire. During term
time, there are performances for school parties every
afternoon Mon–Fri. Public matinees are held at weekends.
From Jun to Aug, Unicorn tours schools, parks and play-
grounds with audience-participation shows. An exciting
range of theatre workshops and activities is open to members of the Unicorn Club.

DRAMA SCHOOL THEATRES

Drama school productions are not always widely advertised
so it may be necessary to make an effort to find out what's
going on. But the effort is worthwhile because standards are
high, seats are cheap, and there is always the possibility of
watching the first public performance of someone who will
one day be a household name. Even Laurence Olivier had to
start somewhere (RADA, actually).

Chanticleer Theatre 1 I 8
Webber Douglas Academy of Dramatic Art, 30–36 Clare-
ville St SW7. 01-370 4154. Finalists from the Webber
Douglas Academy mount productions in the fully equipped
theatre. Wine, fruit juice or coffee before the show or in the
interval. Telephone for details.

Drama Centre
176 Prince of Wales Rd NW5. 01-267 1177. Informal
atmosphere in a large hall with a platform stage. Third year
students engage in workshops and rehearsal exercises, rather
than full productions, usually in Nov, Mar and Jul. Fascinating for those who like to see how the wheels go round.
Unlicensed canteen. *Time Out* for details.

Embassy Theatre
64 Eton Ave NW3. 01-722 8186. Two productions per term
from the students of the Central School of Speech and
Drama in the traditional theatre itself or the small in-the-
round studio. Bar and coffee but no food. Send a s.a.e. for
details.

Guildhall School of Music and Dramatic Art 6 L 30
Barbican Arts Centre EC2. 01-628 2571. The entrance to the

school and its modern, well-equipped theatre (proscenium-arch which is adaptable to thrust or theatre-in-the-round) is in Silk Street, next to the main entrance to the Barbican Arts Centre. Regular performances of drama, opera and musicals with the occasional visiting company outside term time. Bar and snacks. *Time Out* for details.

LAMDA Theatre   1 G 5

Logan Pl, Earl's Court Rd W8. 01-373 7017. Small flexible theatre, with a small bar, where the students of the London Academy of Music and Dramatic Art go through their paces – everything from classics to musicals. In between times, fringe theatre companies sometimes visit. Watch out for posters or send s.a.e. for details.

Mountview Arts Centre

Moutview Theatre School, 104 Crouch Hill N8. 01-340 0097. Mountview is a proscenium-arch theatre, the adjoining Judi Dench Theatre is in-the-round. The students present musicals, music hall, song and dance and drama throughout the year. There is a licensed bar. This one is a club but membership is easy to take out. Look in local paper or telephone for details.

Vanbrugh Theatre Club   3 F 24

Royal Academy of Dramatic Art, 62 Gower St WC1. 01-580 7982. Three theatres – the proscenium-arched Vanbrugh (entrance in Malet St), the flexible G.B.S. and the tiny Studio 13. Here RADA students take their finals in front of an audience. Experimental plays and revivals get the full production treatment. Bar and snack bar. Send s.a.c. for performance details.

ANNUAL EVENTS ———
AND FESTIVALS _____

London is alive with festivals, exhibitions and traditional ceremonies throughout the year, reaching a peak during the summer months. Watch *Time Out*, *What's On* and *City Limits* for information. Here are some of the reliably regular ones that belong under the general heading of arts. Note the special section at the end for events which spread through several months.

January

Park Lane Group. A week in which young and new artists play 20thC music in the Purcell Room on the South Bank. Box office 01-928 3191.

Chinese New Year. A moveable feast in Jan or Feb. Paper lions and dragons prance in the lantern-decked streets of Soho's Chinatown.

February

The English Folk Dance and Song Society has its festival at the Albert Hall. Information from the Society on 01-485 2206.

March

The Camden Festival traditionally offers rare and unusual music, contemporary and classical, in historic buildings around the borough and is widening its scope to include poetry, drama and allied events. Box office 01-388 7727.

Spring Antiques Fair at Chelsea Old Town Hall in King's Rd, SW3. 01-352 2263.

John Stow Memorial Service at St Andrew Undershaft in Leadenhall St EC3. Commemorates the author of *Survey of London*, 1578, basis of all later London histories. The Lord Mayor of London places a fresh quill pen in the hand of Stow's statue (though it has yet to write an appendix). Date can slip into April.

April

Covent Garden Proms. Cheap prom tickets are on sale an hour before the curtain rises on a week of sponsored opera and ballet at the Royal Opera House, 01-240 1066.

London Handel Festival. Professional baroque orchestra and amateur choir present lesser known works in Handel's parish church of St George's in Hanover Sq. Box office 01-828 6913. Date can slip into May.

May

Open Air Art Exhibition at Victoria Embankment Gardens, next to Embankment underground station.

Samuel Pepys Commemoration Service at St Olave's in Hart St EC3. Culminates in the Lord Mayor of London laying a wreath on the monument to the great diarist. Date can slip into June.

June

Antiquarian Book Fair at the Europa Hotel in Grosvenor Sq W1. 01-493 1232. Books, documents, musical scores from international sources.

Charles Dickens Memorial Service at Westminster Abbey on the 9th.

Grosvenor House Fair of antiques and fine art at Grosvenor House Hotel, Park La W1. 01-499 6363.

Greenwich Festival. Amateur and professional arts festival involving most possible venues in the area – concerts at the Royal Naval College Chapel and other historic buildings, events at the theatre, open days in local studios. Box Office 01-317 8687.

Kensington and Chelsea Festival. Music, dance, drama, poetry, paintings – throughout the borough. Information on 01-937 6254.

Richmond Festival. Amateur and professional performing and visual arts, indoor and out. Venues include Richmond Theatre, Orange Tree Theatre, Richmond Green, the Thames. Information on 01-486 9692.

July

Festival of the City of London. Music in St Paul's, the Guildhall, the Livery halls and City churches. Also street theatre, open-air jazz, poetry readings, art exhibitions. Information on 01-377 0540.

Hackney Festival. Drama and music for all heights of brow around the borough, with an emphasis on offerings from ethnic minorities. Information on 01-739 7600.

National Festival of Music for Youth. Young instrumentalists, some still in primary school, give their talents an airing. Details on 01-730 2628.

August

South Bank Summer Music. Popular chamber music and orchestral concerts, jazz and folk, from a concentration of international artists who may not have worked together before. Centred on Queen Elizabeth and Royal Festival halls. Box Office 01-928 3191.

Notting Hill Gate Carnival. The sounds and colour of the Caribbean are created in London's most spectacular ethnic event. Thousands join the West Indian community for a weekend of music, song, dance and street festivities. *Aug Bank Hol.*

September

The Autumn Antiques Fair at Chelsea Old Town Hall, Kings Rd SW3.

October

Burlington House Fair of antiques and fine art at Burlington House in Piccadilly. 01-734 9052.

Early Music Centre Festival presents music from the 12th to 19th centuries played on original instruments. At the Wigmore and Queen Elizabeth halls. Information on 01-251 2304.

National Brass Band Festival. The top brass in contest at the Royal Albert Hall. Box Office 01-589 8212.

November

The Lord Mayor's Procession and Show stretches the rules for inclusion, but is the biggest ceremonial event in the City and a colourful spectacle in a grey month. Second Saturday.

December

Annual Pantomime on Ice at Wembley. Box Office 01-902 1234.

Dr Johnson's Memorial Service at Westminster Abbey on 18th.

Carols in Trafalgar Square around Norway's Christmas present to Britain, a massive pine, richly illuminated.

Summertime Specials

English Bach Festival stages events throughout the year from May at various venues including the Banqueting House, the South Bank concert halls and Sadler's Wells. Information on 01-730 5925.

Open Air Art Shows. Every Sun from May, street artists hang their pictures on the railings along the Green Park side of Piccadilly. And every Sun, pictures, pottery and related objects for the tourists market are on display on the Bayswater Rd side of Kensington Gardens.

Open Air Shakespeare Season from the beginning of Jun to end Aug in Regent's Park Open Air Theatre. Box office 01-486 2431.

Proms. The Henry Wood Promenade Concerts of classical music run from late Jul into Sep. Tickets by ballot for first night and for emotionally-charged last night.

Summer Exhibition at the Royal Academy from May to the end of Jul. The works of contemporary painters, attended by some controversy over selection.

Index

Academy (1 2 & 3) Cinema 37
Africa Centre 22
Agnew Gallery 18
Aldwych Reading Room 65
Alexandra Park 121
All-Hallows-by-the-Tower 93, 117, 118
All Saints 117
All Souls 117
Angela Flowers Gallery 18
Annual Events and Festivals 140–143
Antiquarian Book Fair 141
Antiquarian Bookshops 32–33
Antiques Fairs 141, 142
Apsley House 40
Architecture Libraries 66–67
Art Galleries 5–21
Art Libraries 66–67
Arts Centres 21–29
Arts Council Poetry Library 69
Arts Council Shop 33
Arts Theatre Club 132
Autumn Antiques Fair 142

B2 Gallery 15
Ballet 113–114
Bankside Gallery 15
Banqueting House 41
Barbican Centre 22, 131
Barbican Hall 115
Battersea Arts Centre 24
Battersea Park 121
Bear Gardens Museum and Art Centre 94
Bethnal Green Museum of Childhood 94
Bishopsgate Institute 119
Bloomsbury Central Church 117
Bloomsbury Theatre 132
Bondy Louis, Bookshop 34
Bonham W. & F.C. & Sons, Auctioneers 20
The Book Room, Creative Camera 33
Bookshops 30–36
Bridge Lane Theatre 133
British Architectural Library 66
British Crafts Centre 95
British Film Institute 68
British Library 63–65
British Museum 71
     Department of Prints and Drawings 66
British Theatre Centre 67
Broadcasting Gallery 95
Brompton Oratory 117

Bull and Gate, Pub Theatre 133
Bull's Head Pub 122
Burlington House Fair 142
Bush Theatre 133

Café Theatre Studio 133
Café Theatre Upstairs 133
Camden Arts Centre 15
Camden Centre 115
Camden Festival 141
Camden Institute Poets 126
Camerawork Gallery 125
Carlyle's House 41
Carols in Trafalgar Square 143
Central Hall 115
Central Hall, Westminster 117
Central Music Library 69
Central School of Art & Design Library 66
Chanticleer Theatre 139
Children's Theatre 138–139
Chinese New Year 141
Chiswick House 42
Christie, Manson & Woods, Auctioneers 20
Christie's, South Kensington, Auctioneers 21
Church Farm House Museum 95
Church Music 117–118
Cinema Bookshop 34
Cinemas 36–39
City Lit 126
Classic, Hampstead 37
Classic, Leicester Square 37
Cockpit Theatre 25
Coliseum 113
Collets Chinese Gallery and Bookshop 34
Collets International Bookshop 34
Commercial Galleries 18–19
Commonwealth Institute 25
Compendium Bookshop 30
Concerts 115–117
Conway Hall 115
Courtauld Institute Galleries 13
Courtauld Institute of Art Library 66
Covent Garden Proms 141
Crafts Council Gallery 96
Crane Kalman Gallery 19
Creative Camera, The Book Room 33

Criterion Theatre 129
Crystal Palace Park 121
Cuming Museum 96
Curwen Gallery 19
Curzon Cinema 37

Dance 29, 112–114
Dance Books 34
Design Centre 96
Design Council Slide Library 70
Dickens' House 43
Dickens' Memorial Service 142
Dillons University Bookshop 30
Dingwall's Club 122
Dominion Theatre 122
Donmar Warehouse 133
Drama Centre 139
Drama Library 67–68
Drama School Theatres 139–140
Drill Hall Theatre 134
Dulwich Picture Gallery 13

Early Music Centre Festival 143
Eaton Peter, Bookshop 32
Editions Graphiques 19
Electric Screen Cinema 38
Embassy Theatre 139
English Bach Festival 143
English Folk Dance and Song Society 141
Everyman Cinema 38

Famous Houses 40–63
Fenton House 44
Festival of the City of London 142
Festivals 140–143
Film Libraries 68
Finborough Arms, Pub Theatre 134
Fine Art Auctioneers 19–21
Fine Arts Library 66
Finsbury Circus Gardens 120
Forbidden Planet Bookshop 34
Foreign Patents Reading Room 65
Foundling Hospital 97
Foyles Bookshop 30
French Institute 27
French's Theatre Bookshop 34
Fringe Theatre 132–138

Gala Royal Cinema 38
Garrick Theatre 129
Gate at Notting Hill Cinema 38

Gate Bloomsbury
  Cinema 38
Gate Mayfair Cinema 38
Gate Theatre at the
  Latchmere 134
Gate Theatre at the
  Prince Albert 134
Geffrye Museum 97
Geographia Map Shop 35
Geological Museum 78
Gimpel Fils Gallery 19
Goldsmith's Hall 99
Greenwich Festival 142
Greenwich Park 121
Greenwich Theatre 134
Greyhound Pub 122
Grosvenor House Fair
  142
Grove Theatre 134
Guildhall Art Gallery 16
Guildhall Library 69
Guildhall School of
  Music and Dramatic
  Art 139
Gunnersbury Park
  Museum 99

Hachette Bookshop 35
Hackney Festival 142
Half Moon Pub 122
Ham House 45
Hammersmith Odeon
  122
Hammicks Bookshop 31
Hampstead Theatre Club
  135
Hampton Court Palace 47
Hatchards Bookshop 31
Hayward Gallery 16
Heinz Gallery 14
HMSO Bookshop 35
Heywood Hill G.
  Bookshop 32
History Libraries 68–69
Hogarth's House 50
Holland Park 121
Holy Sepulchre 119
Horniman Museum 100
Hulton Picture Library,
  Radio Times 70
Hyde Park 120

Imperial War Museum 79
Innes Malcolm, Gallery
  19
Institute of Archaeology
  68
Institute of Classical
  Studies 68
Institute of
  Contemporary Arts
  (ICA) 27
Institute of Historical
  Research 69

Jazz Music 122–125
Jewish Museum 100
Jeanetta Cochrane
  Theatre 135
Johnson Dr, House 50
Johnson Dr, Memorial
  Service 143

Joseph E. Bookshop 32

Keats' House 51
Kensington and Chelsea
  Festival 142
Kensington Palace 52
Kensington Pub 123
Kenwood 121
Kenwood House 54
Kew Palace 55
King's Head Pub 123, 135
Kodak Gallery 125
Kodak Museum 101

LAMDA Theatre 140
Lancaster House 56
Latchmere Pub 123
Leighton House 56
Libraries 63–70
Light Fantastic 125
Lincoln's Inn Fields 121
Linley Sambourne
  House 57
Literature Library 69
Little Angel Theatre 138
London Art Bookshop
  35
London Bible Gallery
  101
London Handel Festival
  141
London Library 68
London Toy and Model
  Museum 102
Lord Mayor's Procession
  and Show 143
Lumiere Cinema 38
Lunchtime Music 118–
  119
Lyric, Hammersmith 129

Madame Tussaud's 102
Maggs Bros Bookshop 33
Mall Galleries 16
Manuscripts,
  Department of 64
Map Library 64
Marble Hill House 58
Marlborough Fine Art 19
Marlborough Rare
  Books 33
Marquee Club 123
Martinware Pottery
  Collection 103
Maze Club 123
Mermaid Theatre 135
Minema Cinema 39
Morris William, House
  Gallery 59
Mountview Arts Centre
  140
Mowbrays Bookshop 31
Museum of Garden
  History 103
Museum of Instruments
  107
Museum of London 80
  Library 69
Museum of Mankind 82
Museum of the Order of
  St John 104
Museums 70–112

Music 112–125
Music Libraries 69
Music Library 65
Musical Museum 105

National Army Museum
  85
National Brass Band
  Festival 143
National Festival of
  Music for Youth 142
National Film Theatre 39
National Galleries 5–13
National Gallery 5
National Maritime
  Museum 82
  Library 69
National Monuments
  Record 67
National Museum of
  Labour History 105
National Portrait Gallery 9
National Postal
  Museum 85
National Sound Archive
  126
  Library 68
National Theatre 130
Natural History Museum
  86
New Golden Lion Pub
  123
New Half Moon Theatre
  135
New Inn, Pub Theatre
  136
New Merlin's Cave Pub
  123
Newspaper Library 65
Notting Hill Gate
  Festival 142

Official Publications
  Library 65
Old Red Lion, Pub
  Theatre 136
Old Vic 130
100 Club 123
Open Air Art Exhibition
  141
Open Air Art Shows 143
Open Air Music 119–121
Opera 113–114
Orange Tree, Pub
  Theatre 136
Oriental Manuscripts
  and Printed Books 65
Orleans House Gallery
  16
Osterley Park House 59
Oval House 28

Palaces 40–63
Palladium 130
Pan Bookshop 32
Park Lane Group 141
Parliament Hill 121
Paternoster Square 121
Pavlova Memorial
  Museum 61
Pegasus Pub 123
Penguin Bookshop 32

Pentameters 127
Pepys Samuel,
  Commemoration
  Service 141
Percival David
  Foundation of Chinese
  Art 106
Phillips Auctioneers 21
Photographers' Gallery
  126
Photographic Galleries
  125–126
Photographic Libraries
  70
Pindar of Wakefield, Pub
  Theatre 136
Pizza Express Restaurant
  123
Pizza on the Park
  Restaurant 123
The Place 29
Planetarium 106
Players Theatre Club 136
Poetry 126–127
Poetry Society 127
Polka Children's Theatre
  138
Pollocks Toy Museum
  106
Prince Henry's Room 107
Printing Library 70
Probsthain Arthur & Co,
  Bookshop 35
Proms 143
Pub Theatre 132
Public Record Office
  Library 70
Purcell Room 115

Quaritch Bernard,
  Bookshop 33
Queen Elizabeth Hall 115
Queen's Gallery 17

Radio Times Hulton
  Picture Library 70
Ranger's House 14
Regent's Park 120
Richmond Festival 142
Riverside Studios 29
Robinson & Watkins
  Bookshop 35
Rock Garden Restaurant
  124
Rock Music 122–125
Ronnie Scott's 124
Rota Bertram,
  Bookshop 33
Roxie Cinema Club 39
Royal Academy of Fine
  Arts 17
    Library 67
    Summer Exhibition
      143
Royal Albert Hall 115
Royal College of Music
  116
    Department of
      Portraits 15
    Museum of
      Instruments 107
Royal Court 136

Royal Festival Hall 116
Royal Naval College 116
Royal Opera House 113
Royal Shakespeare
  Company 131
Royal Society of Arts 67

Sadler's Wells Theatre
  113
St Alban Holborn 118
St Botolph Aldgate 118
St Bride 118, 119
St Bride Printing Library
  70
St Bride's Crypt Museum
  108
St George's Elizabethan
  Theatre 137
St George's Gallery,
  Bookshop 35
St Giles Cripplegate 118
St James 118
St James Park 120
St John's 116, 119
St Lawrence Jewry 118,
  119
St Martin-in-the-Fields
  118, 119
St Mary-le-Bow 119
St Mary the Boltons 118
St Mary the Virgin 118
St Mary Woolnoth 119
St Michael-upon-
  Cornhill 118, 119
St Olave 119
St Paul's Cathedral 118,
  119
St Paul's Crypt Museum
  108
St Paul's Steps 121
Sandoe John, Bookshop
  32
Savoy Theatre 131
Scala Cinema 39
Science Museum 87
Science Reference
  Library 65
Screen-on-the-Green 39
Screen-on-the-Hill 39
Second-hand Bookshops
  32–33
Serpentine Gallery 17
Shaftesbury Theatre 132
Shakespeare, Open Air
  Season 143
Shaw Theatre 137
Soane Sir John, Museum
  108
    Library 67
Soho Poly Theatre Club
  137
Sotheby's Parke Bernet,
  Auctioneers 21
Sotheran Henry,
  Bookshop 33
Sound Libraries 68
South Bank Summer
  Music 142
South London Art
  Gallery 18
Southwark Cathedral
  118, 119

Specialist Bookshops 33–
  36
Specialist Cinemas 37–39
Spring Antiques Fair 141
Stanford Map Shop 35
Stanhope Pub 124
Stow John, Memorial
  Service 141
Stratford Poets 127
Studio (1 2 & 3) 39
Summer Exhibition,
  Royal Academy 143
The Swan, Pub Theatre
  137
Syon House 61

Tate Gallery 11
The Temple Church 118
Theatre Royal, Drury
  Lane 132
Theatre Royal,
  Haymarket 132
Theatre Royal, Stratford
  East 137
Theatres 127–140
Torrington Pub 124
Tower of London 109
Tower Place 121
Trafalgar Square, Carols
  143
Tramshed 138
Travis and Emery
  Bookshop 36
Tricycle Theatre 138
Troubadour Poets 127
Truslove and Hanson,
  Bookshop 32

Unicorn Theatre 139

Vanbrugh Theatre Club
  140
Vaudeville Theatre 132
The Venue 125
Victoria and Albert
  Museum 89
    Art Library 67
Victoria Embankment
  Gardens 121

Waddington Gallery 19
Wallace Collection 111
Wembley, Annual
  Pantomime on Ice 143
Wembley Arena 125
Wesley's House and
  Chapel 62
West End Cinemas 37
West End Theatres 128
Westminster Abbey 118
Westminster Abbey
  Treasures 93
Westminster Cathedral
  118
Whitechapel Art Gallery
  18
Wigmore Hall 116

Young Vic 138

Zwemmer A. Bookshop
  36

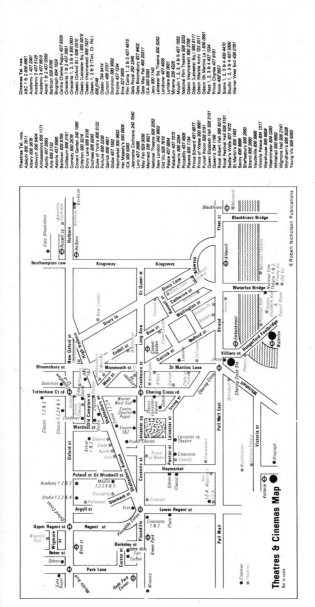

Theatres Tel. nos.

Adelphi 836 7611
Albany 836 3878
Aldwych 836 6404
Ambassadors 836 6111
Apollo 437 2663
Arts 636 2132
Astoria 437 5387
Barbican 628 8795
Barbican 638 3161
Coliseum 836 3161
Comedy 930 2578
Covent Garden 240 1066
Criterion 930 3216
Drury Lane 836 8108
Duchess 836 8243
Duke of York's 836 5122
Fortune 836 2238
Garrick 836 4601
Globe 437 1592
Haymarket 930 9832
Her Majesty's 930 6606
ICA 930 6393
Jeannetta Cochrane 242 7040
Lyric 437 3686
May Fair 629 3036
Mermaid 236 5568
National Theatre 928 2252
New London 242 9802
Old Vic 928 7616
Palace 437 6834
Palladium 437 7373
Phoenix 836 2294
Piccadilly 437 4506
Players 839 1134
Prince Edward 437 6877
Prince of Wales 930 8681
Purcell Room 928 3191
Queen Elizabeth Hall 928 3191
Queen's 734 1166
Royal Albert Hall 589 8212
Royal Festival Hall 928 3191
Sadler's Wells 837 1672
St Martin's 836 1443
Savoy 836 8888
Shaftesbury 836 6596
Strand 836 2660
Vaudeville 836 9988
Victoria Palace 834 1317
Westminster 834 0283
Whitehall 930 6692
Wigmore Hall 935 2141
Wyndham's 836 3028
Young Vic 928 6363

Cinemas Tel. nos.

ABC 1 & 2 836 8861
Academy 1 437 2981
Academy 2 437 5129
Academy 3 437 8819
Astral 1 & 2 437 5359
Barbican 628 8795
Biograph 834 1954
Centre Charles Peguy 437 6339
Cinecenta 1 & 2 437 3561
Cinecenta 1, 2, 3 & 4 930 0631
Classic (Oxford St.) 636 0310
Classic (Leicester Sq.) 930 6915
Classic (Haymarket) 839 1527
Classic 1, 2 & 3 (Tott. Ct. Rd.)
636 6148
Classic 734 5414
Curzon 499 3737
Dominion 580 9562
Empire 437 1234
Eros 327 3839
Film Centa 1, 2 & 3 437 4815
Gate Royal 252 2345
Gate Bloomsbury 837 8402
Gate May Fair 493 20311
ICA 930 6393
Jacey 930 1143
Leicester Sq. Theatre 930 5252
Londoner 437 4606
Lumiere 836 0691
Minema 235 4225
Moulin 1, 2, 3, 4 & 5 437 1653
National Film Theatre 929 3232
Odeon (Haymarket) 930 2738
Odeon (Leicester Sq.) 930 6111
Odeon (Marble Arch) 723 2011
Odeon (St. Martin's La.) 836 0691
Plaza 1, 2, 3 & 4 437 1234
Prince Charles 437 8181
Scene 1, 2, 3 & 4 439 4470
Studio 1, 2, 3 & 4 437 3300
Warner West End 439 0791

Theatres & Cinemas Map

Not to scale

● Cinemas
■ Theatres

© Robert Nicholson Publications

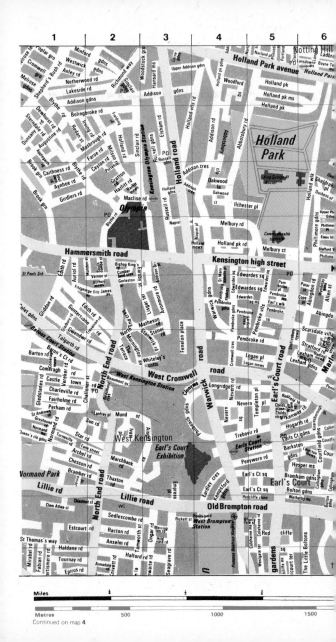

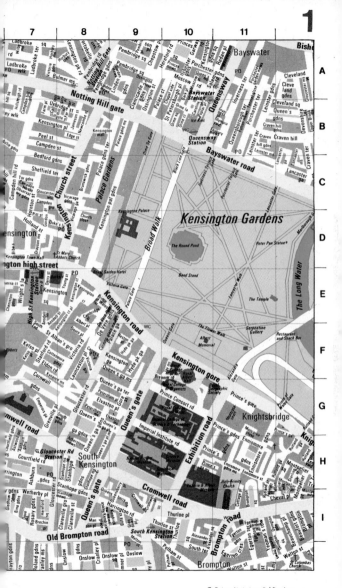

© Robert Nicholson Publications
Crown Copyright Reserved

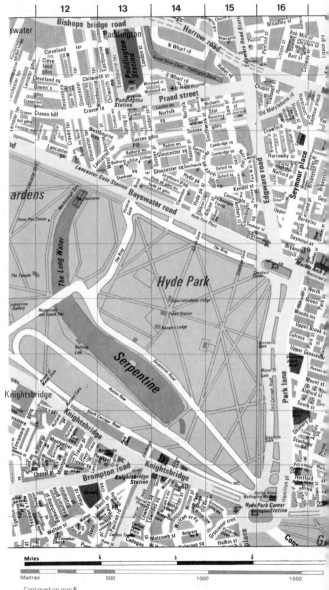

Continued on map **5**

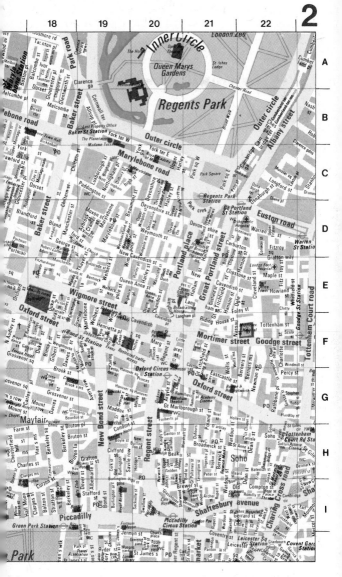

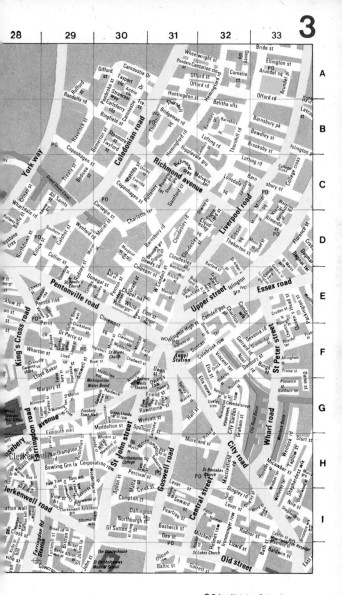

1 2 3 4 5 6

St Thomas's way
Estcourt rd
Racton rd
Anselm rd
Tamworth
Ongar
Station
Princess Beatrice Hosp
Colehern m
Coleherne Red
cliffe
The Little Boltons

Mirabel rd
Haldane rd
Tournay rd
Epirus rd
Shorrolds rd
Fabian rd
Hartismere rd

Westgate ter
Redcliffe gardens

Dawes road
Bishops rd
Burnthwaite rd
Darlan rd

Haldane rd
Armadale rd
Eustace
Kinvert rd
Farm la
Micklethwaite rd
Seagrave rd

Brompton
Cemetery

Finborough rd
Cath
Redcliffe ms
Redcliffe sq
Harcourt ter

Tregunter rd
Cathcart ter
Cathcart rd
Hollywood rd
Seymour rd
Redcliffe rd

Elmstone rd
Shottendane
Harbledown rd

Varston pl
Vereker rd

Walham gro
Farm la
PO

Walham Green
Field rd
cart rd
Faw
Netherton

Novello st
Campana rd
Basuto rd
Favart rd

Effie rd
Cedarne rd
Fulham Broadway Station
Harwood road

Stamford Bridge
Chelsea
Football Ground

Cath
cett st
Redcliffe pl
PO

Fernshaw rd
Gunter gro
Edith gro
Fulham road
St Marks Coll

Fernshaw rd
Edith ter
Starborough
Langton
Netherton

Gertrude st
Lamont rd
Limerston st

Eel Brook
Common
Crondace rd

Musgrave Cres
Kempson rd
Blake gdns
Tyrawley

Moore pk rd
Water
ford rd
Britannia
Maxwell
Rumbold
Holmead rd
Wandon rd

Hortensia rd
Kings road

Edith gro

Worlds End
Pas
Blantyre
Ann

Novello st
Quarrendon rd
Chipstead st
Perrymead st
Bowerdean
Studdridge st

Avalon rd
Harwood rd
Cresford rd
Bovingdon rd
Sandilands rd

Edith
Son ter
End
Smith
Michael rd

Lots rd
Telcott rd
Upcerne rd
Uver dale rd
Tad
Stadium st
Lots rd

Ashburnham rd
Cremorne rd

Clancarty rd
Beltran rd
Ashcombe
Varborough
Friston
Wool
neigh st

Skelbrook ch st
Ryecroft
Bovingdon rd
Pearscroft rd

Fulham Gas Works

Langford
Gilstead rd
Broughton rd
Hazlebury rd
Maynard
Bagley's la
Fulmead rd
Imperial rd
Elswick
st
Elbe st

Dock

Wandsworth bridge road

Canbury
Oxbury
Furness
Stephendale rd
Linden
Eddiscombe
Glanson

River Thames

St Mary's Church
PO
Vicarage cres

Battersea
Battersea wlk
Westbridge rd
Boilegbroke wk
Ranc
clo

Mo

De Morgan
Hamble st
Ashlea st
Edenvale rd
Roseburry rd

Kilvie st
Querrin st
Townmead rd
Fulham Power Station

Granfield
Parkham st
Surrey

Ismailia
rd

Kelnport

Vicarage cres
Lombard
Hannaway
Gwynne rd
Holman
Yelverton rd

Vicarage cres
Orville rd
Battersea High st
Henning
Este rd
Winders rd
Patrick
pass
Simpson st
Bullen st
Home
rd

Croft st
Orbel st
Orbel st
Shuttleworth rd
Inworth st
Batten st
Stanmer st
PO

Surrey
Octavia st
Ursula st
Octavia st

York pl
York pl

Mendip
Chatfield
York road

Philip rd
Hope st
Holgate st
Plough rd
Lavender rd
Ingrave
Mallinson
Fowler cl

Newtoners
Wilton
croft clo
Dagnan rd
Sullivan

Coppock
Patience
McDermott
Hicks clo
Falcon rd
Falcon rd
Khyber rd
Afghan rd
Kerrison rd

Abercrombie st
Eva
Candahar rd
Wayford st
Falcon

Cabul rd
Frere
Row ena cres

Abney
Latchmere

Wynter st
Hibbert
Usk rd
Wallis rd
stanley
Win

Miles

Metres 500 1000 1500

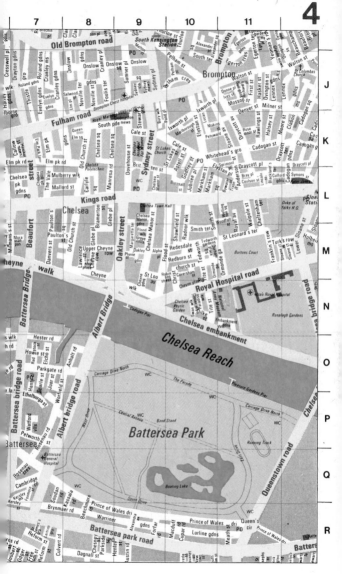

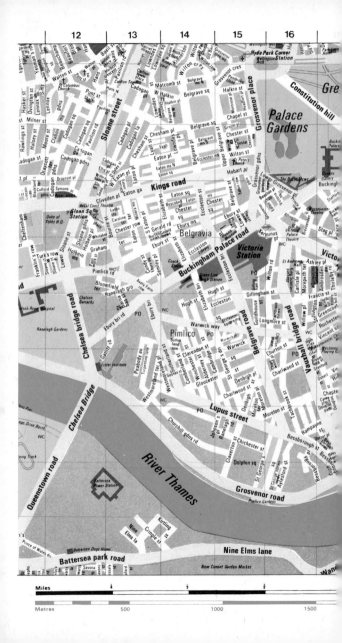

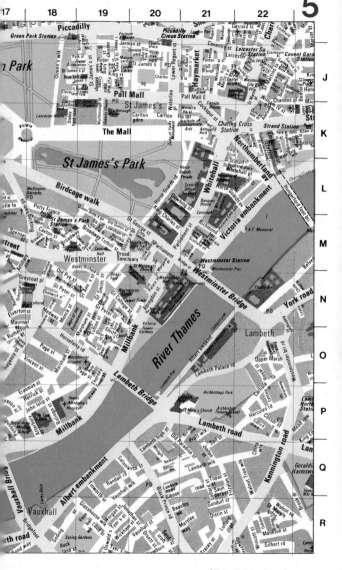

5

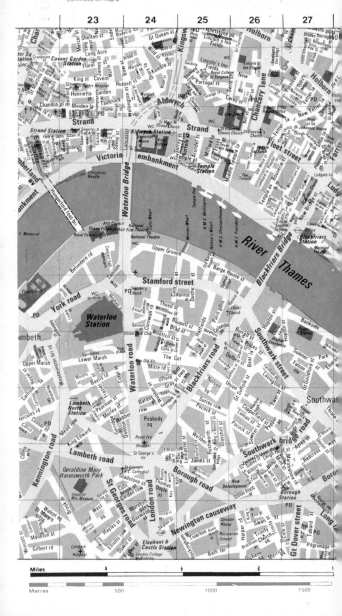